& breakfast

BED &
BREAKFAST

Additional titles in *Entrepreneur's **Startup Series***

Start Your Own

Arts and Crafts Business

Bar and Club

Business on eBay

Business Support Service

Car Wash

Child Care Service

Cleaning Service

Clothing Store

Coin-Operated Laundry

Consulting

e-Business

e-Learning Business

Event Planning Business

Executive Recruiting Service

Freight Brokerage Business

Gift Basket Service

*Growing and Selling Herbs and Herbal
    Products*

Home Inspection Service

Import/Export Business

Information Consultant Business

Law Practice

Lawn Care Business

Mail Order Business

Medical Claims Billing Service

Personal Concierge Service

Personal Training Business

Pet-Sitting Business

Restaurant and Five Other Food Businesses

Self-Publishing Business

Seminar Production Business

Specialty Travel & Tour Business

Staffing Service

Successful Retail Business

Vending Business

Wedding Consultant Business

Wholesale Distribution Business

Entrepreneur
MAGAZINE'S

startup

2ND EDITION

Start Your Own

BED & BREAKFAST

Your Step-by-Step Guide to Success

Entrepreneur Press and Cheryl Kimball

EP
Entrepreneur.
Press

Jere L. Calmes, Publisher
Managing Editor: Marla Markman
Cover Design: Beth Hansen-Winter
Production and Composition: Eliot House Productions

This publication is designed to provide accurate and authoritative information in regard to the subject matter covered. It is sold with the understanding that the publisher is not engaged in rendering legal, accounting or other professional services. If legal advice or other expert assistance is required, the services of a competent professional person should be sought.

Library of Congress Cataloging-in-Publication Data

    Start your own bed and breakfast/by Entrepreneur Press and Cheryl Kimball.—2nd ed.
      p.   cm.
    Includes index.
    ISBN-13: 978-1-59918-149-3 (alk. paper)
    ISBN-10: 1-59918-149-5 (alk. paper)
      1. Bed and Breakfast accommodations—Management. 2. New business enterprises—Management. I. Kimball, Cheryl. II. Entrepreneur Press.
    TX911.3.M27S6986 2007
    910.46'4—dc22   2007026632

Printed in Canada

13 12 11 10 09 08   10 9 8 7 6 5 4 3 2

Contents

Chapter 5

The Roof Over Your Beds:
Legal and Business Structures 69

Chapter 6

The Front Desk: Your Office Start-Up Costs 85

Chapter 7

Fix-Up Central: Purchase, Renovation, and Furnishings Costs

Chapter 8

Getting Up with the Bank: Figuring Your Bottom Line

Preface

You've chosen this book because you're planning to start a bed and breakfast. You'll be living the dream of countless thousands of people—to escape the rat race, renovate and decorate an old home, live where you work while meeting new people and making new friends—and be your own boss.

This is an exciting idea. But it can also be a scary one. You'll be on-call 24/7—much more so than when you worked in the 9-to-5 world. And you'll work long, hard hours, not only greeting guests but cooking and cleaning as well as marketing and bookkeeping. And while you'll be working at home, running the whole show, you'll also be in charge of any and all problems—also 24/7. When you're in charge, you can't turn to someone else to handle questions, problems, and concerns—you're it.

But you're also the one who gets to make all the decisions, bask in the warmth of your guests' praises, and enjoy the rewards of hard work done well. You'll be earning a living doing something you love—and that's priceless.

The Right Answers

You're probably considering becoming a bed and breakfast host, or innkeeper, for one or more of the following reasons:

- You love cooking and entertaining.
- You love remodeling and decorating.
- You have a background in the lodging or hospitality industries and feel this would be an excellent way to combine your experience with a satisfying new career and lifestyle.
- You'd like to supplement your income by putting your home to work for you.

Which did you choose?

It doesn't matter because there is no wrong answer. Any of these responses is entirely correct so long as you realize that they all involve a lot of learning and a lot of hard work. They can also involve a heck of a lot of fun, as well as a tremendous amount of personal and professional satisfaction.

The Goal

Our goal here is to tell you everything you need to know to decide if a bed and breakfast is right for you, and then, assuming it is, to:

- get your B&B and your business up and running
- make your bed and breakfast a success

We've attempted to make this book as user-friendly as possible. We've interviewed lots of people out there on the front lines of the industry—all around the country— to learn the nitty-gritty, hands-on tasks, tips, and tricks to successful B&B innkeeping.

We've set aside places for them to tell their own stories and give their own hard-won advice and suggestions, a sort of virtual round-table discussion group with you placed right in the thick of things. (For a listing of these successful bed and breakfast owners, see this book's Appendix.) We've broken our chapters into manageable sections on every aspect of start-up, production, and promotion. And we've left some space for your creativity to soar.

In this revised edition we've also included a lot more advice on one of the most important tools in today's hospitality industry: the internet and your web site. You'll learn why you need to have a web site and how to design it to make it work hard for you.

We've packed our pages with helpful tips so that you can get up and running on your new B&B as quickly as possible. And we've provided an Appendix crammed with contacts and sources.

So pour yourself a cup of coffee, take a deep breath, turn off the phone, turn off the TV, set your brain to learning mode, and let's go!

The Breakfast
Club

 romantic room for two in a historic home, aglow with the patina of lovingly restored antiques, the luster of fine china, and the sparkle of silver. A fire crackles in the hearth and the rich scents of fresh coffee and homemade cinnamon rolls waft up from the kitchen. It's the picture most people conjure when they consider a stay at a bed and breakfast. And it's an accurate portrait.

But not the only one. Bed-and-breakfast lodgings with a twist are typically found in historic homes, from Revolution-era townhouses to Queen Anne mansions to Craftsman bungalows. But B&Bs also occupy such nontraditional buildings as colonial taverns, 1890s schoolhouses, Roaring '20s banks, Victorian lighthouses, and a panoply of other structures steeped in history and romance. And you'll discover wonderful bed and breakfasts in modern Manhattan high rises, on working dairy farms and cattle ranches, and in many a new home perched beside a river, lake, or the sea.

The quintessential bed and breakfast is located in a seaside hamlet, ski resort, or quaint Victorian village. But you'll also find B&Bs in bustling metropolitan midtowns, desert oases, and classic middle-American small towns.

Best of Both Worlds

What exactly is a bed and breakfast? It's a sort of hybrid between a luxury hotel and a private home, embodying the best of both worlds. A B&B is generally a small establishment with four to ten guest rooms instead of the 50 to 100 or more found at most hotels. The owners live on-site and interact with travelers as if they were invited guests rather than anonymous temporary room numbers. And guests are treated to lots of little deluxe touches like chocolates on their pillows, turn-down service (blankets thoughtfully turned down before bedtime for the pampered guest to slip into), and baskets of bath and beauty products set out on whirlpool tubs.

Of course, there's the "breakfast" in bed and breakfast, a sumptuous home-cooked repast that comes with the price of the room and is served each morning in a communal dining room or in the guest's own quarters. This is not the chain hotel's "continental breakfast" of cold, dry cereal in tiny boxes and sweet rolls wrapped in cellophane, but a morning feast that can range from pancakes made with fresh-picked blueberries to fluffy omelettes stuffed with herbs and cheese to banana breads made from scratch and still hot from the oven.

Bed and breakfasts also tend to feature frosty glasses of iced tea or lemonade on the porch on hot summer afternoons, cups of cocoa after sleigh rides on wintry afternoons, plates of cookies in the kitchen, sherries in the library, or wine and cheese in the parlor on dusky evenings—all a part of the room rate.

Stat Fact
According to Smith Travel Research, in 2005 the average B&B room rate was $90.88, up from $66.65 ten years earlier in 1995.

Popularity Poll

No wonder bed and breakfasts are so popular . . . and becoming more so all the time. According to the New Jersey-based Professional Association of Innkeepers International (PAII, pronounced "pie"), in 1980 there were a relative handful of bed and breakfasts/country inns—1,000 properties that hosted one million guests. In 2004, that number had swelled to 20,000 properties and a $3.4 billion industry.

The Powerful Lure

As you can see, bed and breakfasts are embraced by travelers and entrepreneurs alike. There are as many people who dream of owning that idyllic B&B as there are people who dream of staying in one. More and more vacationers and other travelers choose the bed and breakfast over conventional hotels and motels for the ambience—the comforts of home (not your own hectic one but Grandma's or Great Aunt Nell's old-fashioned one) along with candlelight and romance.

Add in safety and family life. Many travelers, especially single women, feel far more secure staying in a relatively small private home than in a large, impersonal hotel. And many more travelers—men and women—who are frequently away from home on business or other trips relish the feeling of staying with "family" that comes with the B&B and that chain hotels can't hope to provide.

On the other side of the reservations desk, thousands of would-be innkeepers fantasize about owning their own B&Bs. The lure of escaping the 9-to-5 grind to live, work, and play in a beautiful home nestled in a resort or small town is a powerful one. When you can spend your days puttering about in the kitchen or garden, meeting new people, entertaining guests in a lavish and enviable setting, and collect an income while you're at it, who wouldn't leap at the chance?

This is, of course, a fantasy. "People have a romanticized view of the B&B," says Michelle Souza of Nutmeg Bed & Breakfast Agency, a reservation service in West Hartford, Connecticut. The reality involves far more work than guests ever see and most would-be innkeepers ever imagine. But it's still an extremely alluring dream. And it can be a fulfilling reality, if you're willing to work hard to achieve it.

Coffee Cake and Earnings, Too

Besides the basic dream of having your coffee cake and earning a living from it, too, people typically become bed and breakfast owners for the following reasons:

- *To escape the rat race*. Corporate employees who discover that they really don't want to wear a suit every day, report to someone else, let the company set their income rate, and live by the company's rules turn to the bed and breakfast as a way to exercise the management and people skills they've learned while being their own boss. Homebased businesses are becoming more prevalent each year with new entrepreneurs finding new market niches to fill. And what business could be more homebased than the bed and breakfast?

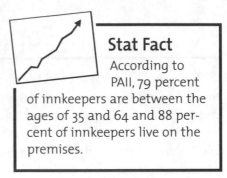

Stat Fact
According to PAII, 79 percent of innkeepers are between the ages of 35 and 64 and 88 percent of innkeepers live on the premises.

- *To supplement income*. People with retirement income find the bed and breakfast a delightful way to add to their earnings while keeping active and expanding their horizons. The B&B can also be a terrific way for younger families to supplement the income of a single breadwinner. Dad—or Mom—can go off to work while the other half stays home with the kids and guests. And many divorced, widowed, or otherwise single people choose to run small B&Bs while working full time as an alternative to taking in a roommate. It not only supplements their income but provides companionship—as often or as infrequently as they choose to host guests.

- *To live in a resort area*. Lots of people dream of living in a ski resort, seaside town, or charming country village, but the reality of trying to earn a living in such an area usually throws cold water on the most fervent ideas. Corporate jobs are few or just plain nonexistent, and service occupations—waitstaff at restaurants, construction worker, lifeguard, or lift operator—are both seasonal and low-paid. So some vacationers who fall in love with a resort area start a bed and breakfast to provide jobs, income, and housing all in one.

- *To purchase a historic home and write off its remodeling costs*. Some people fall truly, deeply, and madly in love with old homes and hear a siren's song to restore them to their former grandeur. This is incredibly expensive. Plaster, paint, woodwork, reproduction hardware and fixtures, not to mention structural shoring up and all those elegant antiques, can require the assets of all of Gringott's Bank. But if you purchase the home with the purpose of converting it to a paying bed and breakfast, you can write off the costs of remodeling and renovation and, eventually, allow the house to pay back those costs and earn revenues.

- *To indulge a love of entertaining*. Some people are born hosts who love nothing more than entertaining guests, regaling them with just the right anecdote for the occasion, serving lavish food and drink, plumping up the pillows, and polishing the silver. For these folks, the bed and breakfast is the ideal venue to showcase their hospitality talents while earning an income at the same time.

Breakfast Perks

One of the perks of running your own B&B is the potential for a sideline business that can neatly tie in with your lodging business. If you're a master gardener, for instance, you might grow flowers, herbs, or vegetables in your backyard. Not only will they be a draw for guests, but you can add to your income by selling them at your local farmer's market. If you're a crafter, you may find that being at home gives you a terrific opportunity to make products to sell at flea markets and art festivals—and, of course, to guests, who'll be fascinated by your talents. And if you've got a commercial-quality kitchen and a flair for baking, you may decide to spend a little extra time at the cooker and turn out cookies, muffins or other delights to sell to local coffeehouses.

All this depends, of course, on your own particular talents, capacity for work, and how busy you'll be with guests. But many innkeepers find that their "hobby" is a wonderful way to earn extra income as well as enchant guests.

The Profit Factor

Whether you'll go into the bed and breakfast business for any or all of these reasons, or for some other reason entirely, is up to you. But no matter what your motivation is, you'll want to know the profit factor. What revenues can you expect as a bed and breakfast host?

The answer varies a great deal, depending on the number of guest rooms in your B&B, the seasonal (or not) nature of your locale, the length of time you're in operation, how creatively you promote your business, and how hard you want to work.

Keep in mind, however, that the bed and breakfast is not a high-income industry. "This is not a business you go into to make a lot of money," cautions Nancy Sandstrom, a former lecturer on B&B start-ups and now in her sixth year as an innkeeper. "You can make a profit, and many of your personal expenses are semi-covered. But it's a lifestyle decision. You'll make your real profit when you sell."

Size Matters

The more guest rooms you have, the more gross income you'll earn. Which makes sense—two rooms at $100 each is $200 per day while ten rooms at the same rate at full occupancy brings in $1,000 per day. Which is great. But it also follows that the more rooms you have, the more expenses and the more work you have as well.

Also note that we've used the term "at full occupancy." No innkeeper, from the most budget-priced mom-and-pop Cheap Sleep Motel to the ritziest five-star Waldorf Hotel, expects year-round total occupancy unless a series of major conventions, the Olympic Games, and a royal coronation are all occurring in town on each other's figurative heels.

> **Fun Fact**
>
> The year 1933 was a bad one for lodging; hotels experienced their lowest-ever occupancy rate of 51 percent, says the American Hotel & Motel Association. And in 1946, with everyone home from the war, the lodging industry had its best-ever occupancy rate of 93 percent.

As the Snow Melts

However, it doesn't all have to be doom and gloom. Not all bed and breakfast locations are seasonal ones. And even if yours falls into that category, there are things you can do to generate off-season traffic. Chapter 11 explores these in-depth, including inventing reasons for guests to visit other than beachcombing or skiing. The seaside B&B might host a Victorian Christmas weekend to bring those summer people in during winter, for example, while the ski resort B&B might feature a Murder Among the Pines mystery weekend to attract tourists during summer.

Building a Reputation

Yet another factor that will influence your occupancy rates and therefore your room revenues is the length of time you're in business. It takes time to build a reputation and a clientele, and you may not see significant revenues for three to five years. This is not true for every B&B, of course; if you locate in an area where demand for lodging outstrips the available choices, your earnings may be high from the outset. And if you choose to purchase an existing bed and breakfast with a good customer base, you can expect higher revenues in your first few years.

The final element in determining your earnings is how hard to you want to work at your business. If you choose to take in guests only seasonally or on alternate weekends, you'll earn less than if you're busily catering to customers 365 days a year.

So, bottom line, what can you expect to earn as a bed and breakfast owner? According to PAII, net income, determined after all business expenses have been deducted, can range from less than $10,000 per year for the small B&B with one to four guest rooms to $80,000-plus for an establishment with nine to 12 guest rooms.

Start-Up Bread

No matter what your profit potential is, you won't have any earnings to count until your B&B is ready to take in guests. And getting up and running takes capital. While you can make do with the extra set of Little Mermaid sheets from your daughter's trundle bed for visiting family and friends, you'll need to buy brand-new bedding for your B&B guests, along with new mattresses, pillows, towels, and more. And even if you'll run your operation from your existing home instead of buying a fixer, local laws may require you to install new kitchen equipment or fixtures, upgrade your pool to public standards or add fire safety fixtures.

Just how much you'll spend will depend, again, on your particular bed and breakfast. Obviously, the fewer guest rooms you have, the fewer mattresses, pillows, towels, and the like you'll have to buy. Also obviously, you'll spend far less updating your existing home with plenty of guest rooms than if you buy a dilapidated relic that was condemned 20 years earlier.

But while it's impossible to put a price tag on the property you'll transform into an inn, it is possible to ballpark renovation and furnishing costs. A good rule of thumb is $35,000 to $50,000 per guest room for larger properties and $20,000 to $40,000 for very small or low-cost operations, according to the PAII.

Fun Fact

Inns tends to set up shop in areas that run-of-the-mill hotels don't find financially feasible, according to the Professional Association of Innkeepers International: 52 percent in small resort villages, 29 percent in rural areas, 16 percent in urban areas, and 3 percent in suburbia.

Host with the Most

Perhaps the most important element to factor in when deciding whether you really want to start a B&B—aside from start-up costs—is whether you've got the personality for the job. Since innkeepers make their work look effortless, most people assume it really is. They imagine a cozy, laid-back lifestyle of greeting guests, chatting before a crackling hearth, and graciously accepting compliments on stupendously prepared gourmet breakfasts.

The reality is getting up every single morning at dawn or earlier to prepare the morning meal, even if you were up all night with a sick child, you have a sinus headache from hell, the regional B&B inspector will be arriving at 10 A.M., and the bank loan officer is expecting an occupancy rate schedule by 11 A.M. Then you've got to serve that breakfast cheerfully and unhurriedly (no yanking plates out from under guests' forks before they're finished) while answering questions about which local sights to take in and how to reach them.

Then there are the dishes to wash, the kitchen to clean, the guest rooms to clean, and laundry to do at the same time you're weeding the garden, taking reservations for next summer, unclogging the toilet in the Scarlett Room's bathroom, and writing advertising copy for the Christmas issues of several magazines. And don't forget about the sick child, the B&B inspector, and the bank!

Multi-Task Master

Innkeeping requires that you be a master of multitasking. It's true that you need to be a people person, one who loves meeting, greeting, and entertaining guests. But you also need to be a front desk clerk, reservations agent, maintenance person, chef, butler, bookkeeper, scullery maid, sales and marketing manager, and housekeeper. And have a life, too.

Fun Fact

Americans are on a weekend getaway whirlwind, says the Travel Industry Association of America. In 2004, 35 percent of all domestic travel was one to two night stays. That was 204 million trips in 2000, up in 2005 to 225 million trips. Continued gas price increases may have an impact, but the chances are greater that people will use a short stay at a bed & breakfast not far from home to satisfy their mini-vacation needs!

The Moderate Squad

Two important elements to consider when deciding whether the B&B business is right for you are its risk and stability factors. Unless you're specifically seeking a money pit to use as a tax shelter (a ploy that doesn't really work anyway), you don't want to pour your heart, soul, and bank account into a venture that's a volatile high risk.

This is not the case with the bed and breakfast. Both risk and stability factors register in the moderate range for this industry. There's an element of uncertainty in starting any new business, but the B&B is considered a stable industry. And since more and more travelers, from honeymooners and businesspeople to seniors, are discovering the delights of bed and breakfast stays every year, the trend seems to be on an upswing and not likely to slow. And that makes the B&B a steady growth opportunity.

If you're a person who likes to stick to one job, do it well for eight hours a day, then go home and leave your work behind, innkeeping is not for you. Sure, a 9-to-5 job is often a drag, but you have the bliss of being able to shut off the lights at the end of the day and call it quits. With a bed and breakfast, you're living "at the office" 24/7, and although you'll have your own private quarters away from the guests, there's no real getting away as long as you're on-site.

"It's really hard work," says Nancy Sandstrom, who with husband Steve runs a six-room B&B in Bayfield, Wisconsin. "In the busy season, you put in 18- to 20-hour days. You're on call all the time."

"Step back and think about the impact on your personal life," warns Michelle Souza of Nutmeg Bed & Breakfast Agency. "This is not a business you can separate from your personal life. And most of it happens on weekends."

"Being an innkeeper is like being a hostess getting ready to have a party every day," says Nancy Helsper, who with husband Charles, runs a 12-room inn in San Diego. "You have to clean the house, prepare the food, and prepare the linens." And be emotionally up. Nobody wants a host who's dragging or cranky.

If you love being on the go all the time, accomplishing several tasks at once—even on 50 consecutive weekends—and creatively meeting new challenges while also carrying on cheerfully at drudge work, then you'll be in your element as a B&B host.

All Inn the Family

But there's still more to being a bed and breakfast innkeeper. You'll have guests in your home at all times. And while you may (or may not) get away with Pokémon cards strewn across the living room, a layer of dust on the dining room table, and various assortments of dirty laundry lining the hallway when Mom comes to visit, you can't do so with paying guests. They'll expect to see a charming, clean, and tidy showplace at all times. So if you—and your family—are more into sailing along through a sea of stuff than in keeping things shipshape, you'll have a tough time with a B&B.

Which brings us to a very important point. Unless you're a single person who'll be sole owner and the only permanent resident of your bed and breakfast, you'll need to consider the personalities of your significant other or spouse and family as well as your own. Living in a B&B is the same as having nonstop house guests; it means you have to give up a certain amount of privacy. You can't wander around in your skivvies any time you like or sweat along with that step aerobics video in the den. And unless you're careful to confine all conversation to your private quarters, everything from planning sessions on planting the garden to heated discussions on whether your daughter is allowed to get her nose pierced, may be staged in front of complete strangers.

If your family is basically friendly, cheerful, and outgoing, they'll enjoy the interaction with guests as much as you will. But if they're not social butterflies, or simply are uncomfortable with the idea of sharing their home with strangers, you may find yourself in deep and difficult waters. While most B&B families have a ball in the business, some innkeepers found that it made their families so unhappy they had to give it up.

Smart Tip

"There are two parts to being a successful host," says Nancy Helsper, co-owner of a Queen Anne mansion B&B in San Diego. "There's innkeeping—being a concierge and hostess—and there's the business side: taxes, payroll, and marketing."

Industry Nightmares

Besides keeping track of everything from chocolates on pillows at bedtime to fresh flowers in the dining room to which guests are allergic to eggs, innkeeping demands that you also be extremely organized and detail-oriented.

If you're a cheerful but scattered type who trusts that book work will take care of itself, you'll soon find yourself in one of the hospitality industry's nightmares: having overbooked by reserving the same room for two (or more) sets of guests at the same time. Or forgetting that the Smythes never sent in their deposit to hold

The Innside Story

Surf through the Professional Association of Innkeepers International's web pages or the pages of B&B publications, and you'll find lots of training programs, workshops, and seminars. Some are weekend workshops that deal with specific issues like marketing; others are complete hands-on week-long sessions that let you take the host driver's seat and learn innkeeping on-the-job.

Take a course or two before you purchase your property or start renovations. You'll handle everything from reservations and greeting guests to preparing rooms and meals. It's a good way to discover what innkeeping really entails and find out whether you've got what it takes—and whether you'll like it.

their room during the biggest holiday weekend of the year. Which means that they never show up and neither does anyone else because you held the room for the Smythes.

You also must be able to keep a stern and steady watch on your supplies and your bookkeeping. Your guests won't be impressed if you run out of toilet paper, forget to buy eggs for next morning's meal, or don't have clean sheets because you overlooked paying the laundry service.

The Right Stuff

The people we interviewed for this book come from a variety of backgrounds. Two are long-timers in the hospitality business, one is a TV executive and another is retired military. What they all have in common is the right stuff—an ability to combine the skills and enthusiasm they acquired in other careers and apply them to the formidable—but fun—task of running a bed and breakfast.

Love at First Site

David and Marilyn Lewis, of Fort Worth, Texas, didn't start out with the idea of running a bed and breakfast. Two years ago, they were cruising neighborhoods, looking for a house to remodel, when they came across the 1893 mansion that's now their inn. "It had been vacant for 12 years and was sitting here crumbling," Marilyn says. But the couple saw through the neglect to the beauty beneath—it was love at first sight and seemed to provide a serendipitous way to put their talents, and the house, to work as a B&B.

"Everything we've done in our lives prepared us to do this," Marilyn, an interior decorator, explains. "We like people. I like to cook and decorate and entertain. It was all just natural." But it's also a lot of work. "Nobody should ever do a B&B if they think it's easy," Marilyn says.

The couple moved in, setting up housekeeping in an apartment at the back of the main house—although the term "apartment" could be used loosely. "It had no plumbing or anything," Marilyn recalls. "We moved in and thought, 'This is a money pit. How are we going to pull this off?'"

Pull it off they did—with resounding success. David, an executive with a Christian cable TV network and an ordained minister, and Marilyn decided to use love and romance as their theme. First they remodeled the carriage house, turning it from what Marilyn calls "one step up from homeless" into two hearts-and-flowers suites. The Beloved Cottage was up and running in just eight months, and the Sweetheart Cottage followed six weeks later. "We put up our web site," Marilyn says, "and another bed and breakfast in town (there are only about five) sent us their overflow."

Besides the main house and cottages, the inn also includes four corporate apartments in two duplexes across the street. The couple's daughter lives in one unit; the others fill with corporate people in midrelocation or traveling, and also act as overflow for the cottages on weekends. There's still a long way to go. The main house, which will have four guest rooms, was still in the throes of major renovation when we interviewed the couple.

But with romance as its theme, in just 18 months in business, the inn has hosted 91 honeymoon couples, David says proudly, along with about 150 anniversary couples and many birthdays and getaways.

Twenty Reasons Why

Like David and Marilyn, Nancy and Steve Sandstrom of Bayfield, Wisconsin, fell in love with their house and knew they had to have it. Unlike their Texas counterparts, however, the Midwest couple had already decided to open a bed and breakfast. They just hadn't decided where or when. "Steve was part-owner of a family printing company," Nancy says. "I had 15 years [of experience] as an executive director and marketing director for nonprofit corporations. It was empty nest time, with one child in college and one about to be. We'd had enough of corporate life; we were emotionally and psychologically ready."

The couple had been conducting market research for three years—and taking their time about taking the plunge—when Nancy ran into old friend Jerry Phillips of PAII at the association's 1995 annual conference. Jerry, who owns an inn nearby, told Nancy the house that's now her B&B was for sale. "I gave him 20 reasons why buying it was a bad idea," Nancy recalls, "and finished up with, 'How much do they want for it?'" She then called husband Steve, and they decided to go for it.

And with good reason. The 1885 sandstone house, nestled in the woods along Pikes Creek and with views of Lake Superior, had been in Nancy's family from 1905 until it was sold in 1994 to a couple who turned it into a two-room B&B. It's three miles south of Bayfield, a quaint lakeshore community that's a destination resort for the region. "It's one of the most beautiful places in the Midwest," Nancy says contentedly. "I've spent every summer of my life here."

The house had been in operation as a B&B for years, but without much success. The old

Stat Fact

What are the most popular travel times for Americans? Summer, fall, and spring, with winter being the least popular says the Travel Industry Association of America.

> ## Tip...
>
> ## Smart Tip
>
> A well-honed sense of humor is an important part of the innkeeper's arsenal. If you can't laugh when the inevitable predicaments occur, you won't last long.

owner had kept no financial records to help guide Steve and Nancy, and the house itself needed lots of TLC. "When we bought the property it was in terrible shape," Nancy explains. "Structurally it was OK, but mechanically and cosmetically it needed a lot."

Six years and a lot of hard work later, the house gleams with the patina of care and attention—to the delight of its many guests. Nancy ran the inn by herself for the first two and a half years, while Steve wound down his career in the city. He still works full time away from the B&B but much closer to home, so he can share in the innkeeping duties (and pleasures).

Steve and Nancy expanded the B&B from the four guest rooms it had when they purchased it in 1996 to five guest rooms and a third-floor suite. With relaxation and the great outdoors as their keywords for guests, they're booked solid all summer season as well as during winter's blustery weather.

Air Force to Farmhouse

Bill and Sandra Wayne began looking into the B&B business in 1982 ("seriously in 1984," Bill says), and when he retired from the U.S. Air Force in 1986, the couple started in on Sandra's 80-acre ancestral farm, which they had acquired five years earlier. "The farm was placed on the National Register of Historic Places in 1994 as the John A. Adams Farmstead Historic District because of pioneering soil conservation practices by Sandra's great-grandfather," Bill says.

Located seven miles from Warrensburg, Missouri—about an hour southeast of Kansas City—the B&B encompasses two separate buildings. "The 1867 Farmhouse suite includes five rooms of the original farmhouse," Bill explains. "The Cottage on the Knoll is a secluded, romantic cottage with a whirlpool tub, fireplace, and king bed. We live in a 700-square-foot addition to the farmhouse—three rooms, plus a laundry area for the two of us."

Transforming the property into the family and romance-themed B&B it is today took hard work as well as imagination. "From 1986 to 1988, we renovated the farmhouse by adding a modern addition for our quarters and to provide a place for HVAC (heating, ventilation, and air-conditioning), indoor plumbing, and the like," Bill says. "The architecture in a 120-year old house limited what we could do, so we started with two rooms with a shared bath."

The couple later changed their marketing strategy to make the two rooms into a suite that's perfect for families and other groups. "In 1998, we built the cottage to our own design," Bill adds. With horses and barn swallows in the old barns—in constant use since the 1870s—and wild turkeys and deer roaming around outside, the B&B offers guests the best of country pleasures and city amenities.

Seaside Seasons

Halfway across the country, on northwest Florida's Emerald Coast, Bruce and Judy Albert are celebrating their inn's 13th year in business—it opened in 1990. "We have been in the hospitality business most of our lives," Bruce and Judy say.

And it shows in their choice of location for the Georgian plantation-style B&B. "The inn is located less than a one-block walk to the Gulf of Mexico and just a few steps to the town center of Seaside," the couple explains. "This was the filming location for the movie, *The Truman Show*, starring Jim Carrey. During the season—all spring, summer, and fall—there are movies in the park, storytellers, wine festivals, ballets on stage in the Lyceum, classical, country, jazz, easy-listening, and rock 'n' roll concerts.

"The inn has seven rooms, each with private bath, wet bar, TV, VCR, telephone, clock-radio, and fireplace, and two suites with private baths, living rooms, and butler's kitchens," the innkeepers say. The same amenities, from TV to fireplace, are provided in the larger settings as well.

"Our living quarters are off-premises," Bruce and Judy say. "We live on a farm where we grow pesticide-free vegetables, edible flowers, herbs and fruits, which we bring to the inn as often as possible for the breakfasts and dinners we serve."

Although the bed and breakfast looks as if it's been a regal member of its seaside community for more than a century, it was built a mere 13 years ago—and acts as a showcase for Bruce and Judy's considerable talents. "We serve breakfast every morning in our cozy 18-seat dining room," the couple says. "We are open for lunch and dinner on a seasonal basis. We are the host year-round for many bridal showers and weddings."

With its Southern charm and stunning Emerald Coast location, the inn is sure to do well into the next century—and beyond.

Kismet

A world away in San Diego, Nancy and Charles Helsper, married just one year, were looking for an antique four-poster bed and found instead an entire bed and breakfast inn. And like David and Marilyn in Fort Worth, they fell instantly in love with the place. Nancy

Fun Fact

The pancake—that staple of the American hot breakfast—first came into being many centuries ago in England and is still a Shrove Tuesday tradition in that country. Cooks looking ahead to Lent, when dairy products were prohibited, used their stores of butter, eggs, and milk to make, and then merrily eat, pancakes by the score.

was working as assistant director of catering at the San Diego Hilton, and Charles was safely ensconced in his second career—after the Navy—with General Dynamics. The couple had taken a PAII aspiring innkeeper course with the idea of moving back East and opening a B&B when they retired. But that was years in the future—they thought.

Then came the phone call. "A friend called and said she'd read in the paper that a bed and breakfast in Old Town San Diego was being liquidated and holding an estate sale," Nancy recalls. "It was only five blocks from our home, and we didn't even know it was a B&B."

Nancy and Charles went to take a look at the furniture, saw the Queen Anne mansion and decided then and there to buy it. It was kismet! But the owner insisted the house was in bankruptcy and couldn't be sold. Nancy and Charles, however, were determined. They called the owner in the middle of the night and persuaded her to negotiate a sale, a complicated procedure because the building was on a lease from the county.

"We purchased the lease," Nancy says. "But we had to purchase all the furnishings as well, and they'd already been advertised." Which meant they had to let in the public. "The owner gave me a five-minute start before she opened the doors. I ran around and wrote 'Sold' on everything."

The same morning—as so often happens when fate decides to lend a helping hand—Nancy was promoted to director of catering, a position for which she'd worked long and hard. Even though she was now an innkeeper, Nancy felt she couldn't turn down the promotion. So she and Charles worked full time at outside jobs and ran the inn, with the assistance of the manager they'd inherited with the property.

The couple decided to keep their home. "We had a dog, and Charles wanted us to have our own space," Nancy says. So when Charles got laid off less than three months later and Nancy had left her job, they were suddenly down from two and a half incomes (the half being the Navy pension) to just one-half, and two mortgages.

A giant gulp. But Charles and Nancy made it work. They transformed the inn into a showplace for business as well as leisure travelers with private baths for each room (initially baths were shared) and phones in all rooms. They purchased the Italianate villa next door. And they both worked at the inn until they could afford staff.

All the long hours and financial investment paid off. Now with 12 guest rooms or suites, the inn has just celebrated its ninth anniversary and boasts an enviable 80 to 85 percent occupancy rate year-round.

Breakfast Forecast

After you've considered start-up costs, potential profits, and whether you've got the moxie for the job, one final issue to consider is the forecast for the bed and breakfast industry. Is the B&B concept a fad or a form of lodging that's here to stay?

The forecast is excellent. Bed and breakfast is in a steady growth stage, predicts PAII. Twenty-five percent of guests are first-timers to B&Bs, a figure that indicates there's a still large market out there to be tapped. Innkeepers are adding guest rooms because they have a need for them rather than in a desperate ploy to increase revenues. They are also upgrading existing rooms to meet guests' needs, not merely because of perceived trends. The bed and breakfast industry tends to be recession-proof. In a down economy, travelers may

Fun Fact

In the 1993 comedy flick, *Groundhog Day*, Bill Murray and Andie McDowell stay in a bed and breakfast—over and over and over again.

not be able to swing the price tag of a European vacation or Caribbean cruise. But the B&B that's perhaps no more than two to four hours from home is still an affordable luxury, and therefore more of a buy than ever in a down economy. In an up economy, the bed and breakfast's deluxe amenities and personal pampering keep it a desirable lodging destination.

All of which makes the B&B the way to go for the entrepreneur who wants the joy and fascination of meeting new people and the satisfaction of making folks feel pampered while working at home in a challenging environment.

So let's get started! Pop those cinnamon rolls in the oven, pour yourself a fresh cup of java, and get going with B&B 101.

B&B
101

OK, you're already planning what sort of historic mansion you'll buy or how you'll remodel your own home to make it a stellar bed and breakfast. You're surrounded by cookbooks, paint swatches, and fabric samples. You're on a roll.

Great! But there's a lot to learn before you're ready to greet your first guests. So don your chef's or carpenter's apron and step into the classroom of B&B 101.

B&B Chronicles

Although the bed and breakfast, at least in the United States, seems new and trendy, it's not—it goes back a long way. Inns, as everyone who's ever heard the story of Mary and Joseph's travels to Bethlehem knows, go back as far as recorded history.

Inns studded the Roman roads in ancient Britain but faded out during the Middle Ages, when travel was a risky business. If you traveled at all during those dark days, you were put up at monasteries where you were fed, housed, and given something to drink. (Monks developed many famous liqueurs, including Benedictine.) Gradually, however, inns resurfaced—although not as the gracious and genial hostelries you might imagine. You were expected to provide not only your own breakfast and other victuals but also your own bedding.

Eventually life for the British traveler improved. By the 16th century, inns were more or less as we recognize them today. And by the middle of the 17th century, inns had become important stops along coach routes—because coaches provided the only real public long-distance transportation.

George Washington Slept Here

The first American inns, modeled on their home country counterparts, sprang up at Atlantic seaports and—just as in many a modern B&B—converted farmhouses along stagecoach routes. These, of course, were the quintessential lodgings of New England (or at least their prototypes), the storybook versions that pop into everyone's mind when you utter the words "country inn," the myriad hostelries George Washington purportedly slept in.

As George won the war and the nation grew, so did the face of its lodgings. Hotels mushroomed along with commerce, but they were either deluxe accommodations with matching price tags or budget-priced and, frankly, grim. Every small town and many an urban neighborhood had its tourist or guest house for those who couldn't afford the luxury hotel and preferred to share breakfast and supper in a family atmosphere than take their chances at the local diner.

When automobiles became de rigueur, motor courts and then motels began to dot the landscape. The first of these appeared in always

Fun Fact

During the great age of coach travel in England, coach terminals or "stages" were customarily found at inns.

progressive California in 1925, and by the late 1950s, motels had become major rivals of hotels and any other sort of lodging establishment for the affections of traveling Americans. You could choose from mom-and-pop places with Peter Pan, Sputnik, or cowboy themes, or snazzy franchise operations like Howard Johnson's. Instead of having to tip armies of bellboys and doormen, you could drive right up to your room, disgorge your passengers and luggage, and then dive into the swimming pool conveniently located on the other side of the parking lot.

Which was cool for a lot of years. But by the 1970s, Americans had grown weary of formulaic motels and even hotels, where everything from the dressers to the bedspreads (orange and brown) to the prints on the walls looked exactly the same. The ice machine at the end of the corridor, the Coke machine at the bottom of the stairs, and the Formica lobby lined with racks of brochures had lost their charm.

And thus the bed and breakfast—the updated tourist house and downscaled country inn—was born. Or actually reborn. B&Bs have been a staple of the hospitality industry in Europe. In Britain, they're called bed and breakfasts; in Italy, pensiones, and in Germany, zimmer frei. But they're all the same thing—unique and cozy lodgings serving both breakfast and a place to stay.

Bed, Breakfast, and Electricity

America's idea of acceptable travel accommodations has evolved over the years along with the lodgings themselves. The first great innovation came along in 1908 with Ellsworth Statler's flagship hotel in Buffalo, New York, which featured private baths for all rooms. The Statler chain set the standard for moderately-priced hotels—previously an unknown entity—for decades to come. Only a few years later, new hotels boasted electricity but still provided candles and matches in every room. (You couldn't quite trust that new-fangled light source.)

In 1934, the Statler chain led the way again by providing air conditioning in its public rooms, but it wasn't until 1940 that you could routinely expect to find air conditioning in the guest rooms of most hotels. The first in-room coffee service didn't show up until the mid-1950s, and it was almost the Kennedy era before you could expect TV and direct-dial phones in every room. The mini-bar, that staple of the moneyed guest in love with junk food, arrived on the scene in the early 1960s, and in-room movie channels made their debut in 1976, just in time for the nation's bicentennial. Imagine what George Washington would have thought of all these amenities!

While a bed and breakfast is by definition a lodging that serves breakfast as part of the room rate, there are several different types of B&B properties ranging from intimate family homes with less than a handful of guest rooms to full-fledged country inns with a dozen or more rooms. Part of the charm of B&Bs is that each is a bit different, but they all fall somewhere within one of these basic categories:

> **Fun Fact**
>
> During colonial times, says *The Waiter's Digest*, seaport taverns offered hooks in the back room from which weary sailors could hang their hammocks, pricier places offered bunks.

- *Homestay*. This is essentially a private home with one to four guest rooms that are used to bring in supplemental rather than primary income, a sort of variation on the high school foreign-exchange student theme where guests absorb the true flavor of staying with a family. Homestay hosts generally feel that of all the bed and breakfast models, only theirs provides the "authentic" B&B experience, the one for which their guests seek them out. Homestays don't typically post signs on their properties or advertise, relying instead on reservations services. They're usually exempt from zoning, health, and other government regulations. A homestay is also called a host home.

- *Bed and breakfast*. A step up from the homestay, the B&B typically consists of four or five (but as many as eight) guest rooms and a live-in owner or host family. The difference between this model and the homestay—aside from the number of rooms—is that the bed and breakfast typically has a sign out front, advertises, and conforms to zoning, health, and other government requirements.

- *Bed and breakfast inn*. This is the Bob Newhart version, a full-fledged lodging establishment rather than a family home with rooms to let. With six or more guest rooms and a live-in host, the B&B inn has a well-posted sign, does lots of advertising, and adheres to all government regulations.

- *Bed and breakfast hotel*. Technically, this one isn't really a B&B at all; it's a hotel with 30 or more rooms that happens to be located in a historic building. Capitalizing on the B&B craze, it offers breakfast as part of the room rate.

- *Unhosted apartment or cottage*. This is a sort of cross between the vacation rental and the B&B. Anything from a swanky uptown apartment to a cottage in the woods, it's a self-contained lodging, completely separate from the host's home. Breakfast is usually stashed in the fridge or delivered each morning in a basket; aside from that, guests are left on their own. B&Bs of various types also often include hosted cottages, carriage houses, and other separate but on-site buildings, and breakfast is either delivered to the door or guests stroll across the grounds to the dining room.

In this book, we use the terms "bed and breakfast," "B&B" and "inn" interchangeably as well as the words "host" and "innkeeper." (And of course, a host can equally well be a hostess!)

With Reservations

No matter what type of B&B you plan to run, you'll need guests to fill your rooms. And while most bed and breakfasts (except for homestays) rely on advertising and marketing, just like businesses in other industries, they also land guests in a unique fashion. And that's with the reservation service organization (or RSO).

This "matchmaker" agency is the method of choice for homestay hosts but is employed by larger properties as well. Here's how it works:

1. Owners list their properties with the RSO. This entails writing up an enticing description of the property and providing photos. Most RSOs also require an inspection so they know you meet their standards and criteria.

2. The RSO publishes the description and photos on its web site and/or guidebook and advertises it—along with its other properties—in magazines and other venues.

Fun Fact

The picturesque country inn run by TV characters Dick and Joanna Loudon in the popular 1980s sitcom, Newhart, really exists. Only the exterior of the historic Waybury Inn in Middlebury, Vermont, was ever seen, however. The interiors were all Hollywood sets.

Inn Country

People often confuse the country inn and the bed and breakfast inn, but they're not the same thing. Perhaps the biggest difference between the two is that the country inn features an on-site restaurant serving dinners or even lunches in addition to the quintessential breakfasts.

Some country inns (which can be in urban locations, too) include dinner along with the morning meal as part of the room rate; others provide it as an option. And you don't have to be a guest to partake of the gourmet cuisine; country inn restaurants are usually open to the public.

Country inns can also be quite a bit bigger than the B&B inn, with as many as two dozen or more rooms, and usually have a manager to handle operations instead of a live-in owner/host.

3. Prospective guests call the reservation service, which then matches up guests and hosts, making suggestions if the guest doesn't have a specific property in mind and also handling issues like kids, pets, and smoking preferences.

4. Once the match is made, the RSO makes the reservation, takes and processes the deposit and payment, sends a reservation confirmation to the guests, and gives them directions to the B&B.

5. Last but certainly not least, the RSO sends the deposit and payment—less a commission of typically 20 percent—to the host.

The beauty of all this for the host is that she doesn't have to bother with either advertising or processing credit card deposits and payments, which can be expensive, especially for the supplemental income innkeeper. And for the homestay, which because of its residential zoning status doesn't have—or want—a sign on the front lawn and strangers dropping in at all hours, the reservation service provides a sort of virtual visibility.

What happens if you sign up with a reservation service and then make some bookings on your own? Nothing (unless you make the mistake of overbooking). You only pay commissions on reservations made by the service. (Be sure, however, to check this issue with individual RSOs before you sign on the dotted line.)

There are regional as well as national and international reservation services. Typical costs, in addition to the commission on each booking, range from $15 to $75 per year. Some services also require an initial membership fee in the same range, and many require that you carry a certain amount of liability insurance. While some agencies simply handle bookings, others function as industry associations, providing political advocacy, group buying power, public relations, and screening of prospective guests.

"I help guide new hosts through the maze of bureaucratic requirements," says Ruth Young of Mi Casa Su Casa, an RSO in Tempe, Arizona, that lists about 300 properties in the southwestern U.S. as well as a couple of villas in Spain and Mexico. "If they have questions about insurance, linens, telephone service, guest food allergies, quiet hours, diet oddities, recipes, disabled requirements, types of preferred beds, soaps, chemical allergies, or whatever, I try to give them my best advice or point them in helpful directions."

Michelle Souza of Nutmeg Bed & Breakfast Agency also feels a large part of her job is helping the novice host get up and running with ease. "We'll work with you to set prices and understand market nuances in your area. We help you get into business immediately."

Stat Fact
Traveling is a fairly safe activity. According to the Travel Industry Association of America, crimes against travelers occur 40 percent less often than crimes against stay-at-homes.

Sheryl Brecker and Suzanne London of Bed & Breakfast Reservations in Gloucester, Massachusetts, agree: "We offer consultation services on most aspects of starting and running a B&B."

But that's not all a good RSO can do for you. "We screen potential guests to ensure the best possible match between guest, host, and specific accommodation," Brecker and London explain. "This means we let the host know some basic information about a guest, why they are coming, and what interests they might have when they get to the area."

"I see the properties I book, so I can tell prospective guests things they can't learn by reading a guidebook or talking to the owner," Souza explains. She can compare the pluses and minuses of various B&Bs as they apply to that particular guest—for example, helping a guest weigh the differences between an inn that's closer to a relative's home than another that serves a preferred vegetarian menu. "I can be objective, and I can be the bad guy," Souza adds. "Which is tough to do when you own the property." You may find it difficult to just say no to smokers or pets, but for Souza it's a snap. It's her job.

The Screening Room

Screening is an important consideration for many hosts—especially newbies who aren't sure what sort of guests to expect—and helps them feel safer about the folks they're inviting into their homes. What does the screening process consist of? "The first question is are they nonsmokers or will they smoke outside," says Ruth Young. "Then, depending upon their personality and time pressure (some professionals have a minimum amount of time, like emergency room physicians, or businesspeople calling in between flights), we ask for their name, address, home phone, work phone, name of the person(s) coming with them, age of children and their genders and names.

"We ask what kind of B&B they enjoy," adds Young, whose company has been in operation since 1981, "[a place] with one or two guest rooms, an inn with five to 21 guest rooms, or a separate, free-standing guest house. Would they like any special amenities, like a heated spa or pool, a tennis court, double whirlpool tub, fireplace, or DSL connection for their computer? We ask if they need to be in any special area of a city (in other words, are you coming for a business meeting or convention, visiting relatives, coming for a wedding, funeral, etc.). Usually, we ask about their occupation so we can semi-introduce them to their hosts, their airlines, and flight numbers, so the hosts can check to see if the flights are on time. Or, if they're driving, what their probable time of arrival is. We ask if they have any allergies to food or pets and if they have any food preferences.

"By the time we find out the above," Young counsels, "and ask for their credit card for the total amount if one day, or 50 percent of three or more days, and ask them to pay the balance due upon arrival in cash, business, or personal check—or traveler's

checks if the host does not take credit cards—we feel like we know our guests pretty well. We have never had a bad check, and we have never had any theft."

Minks and Umbrellas

All this screening works both ways. Young's Mi Casa Su Casa, like all reputable RSOs, also screens hosts and conducts home inspections to make sure prospective B&Bs are up to the agency's standards.

"I am very careful about who I accept as hosts, as you might imagine," says Young. "I don't accept everybody who wants to be a host. I am very aware of their residential neighborhood, the look of their house, their friendliness, and hospitality. Do they offer me refreshments? Do they have table settings out? Do they have a sense of humor? I consider the decor so I can describe it to guests. And I always sit on the beds. I observe their pets' behavior around a stranger. Do they have too many personal effects in the guest room or bathroom? Guests don't appreciate a lot of family pictures in the bedroom or not having space in the bathroom to lay out toiletries. How about the privacy factor?" As a follow-up to screenings and placements, Young sends out evaluation cards to guests.

"The kitchen and bath are the primary criteria for approving an accommodation, regardless of all other aspects," Brecker and London of Bed & Breakfast Reservations say. "For example, an accommodation with fancy modern-day amenities may not be approved if cleanliness issues are found on inspection, while a simple B&B host home, even with a shared bath, would be approved if immaculate as long as other inspection criteria are met. Also, if pets are in the residence, are there cleanliness issues related to pets?"

"Every place is so different," says Young. "It's fun for me, matching guests with hosts and having both very happy. We've had guests so pleased that they've brought flowers or candy, taken their hosts to dinner, invited hosts to their homes, Cape Cod beach houses, and more. Hosts have offered their guests umbrellas, sweaters, even a mink coat when it turned very chilly, and the guests were going to a bar mitzvah."

Rating the RSO

So how do you choose which reservation service to go with? Perform your own screening. Since you'll be parting with 20 percent or more of each booking as well as relying on the

Tip...

Smart Tip

An RSO's host screening also covers issues such as those described by Sheryl Brecker and Suzanne London of Bed & Breakfast Reservations in Gloucester, Massachusetts: electrical, lighting, handrails, smoke detectors, fire extinguishers, and anything that might be in the "accident waiting to happen" category.

RSO to send you paying customers, you'll need to go with an agency you can trust and with which you can develop a rapport. Important points to consider include the amount and quality of the agency's marketing and promotions, the specific services it offers to members, and its hours for telephone reservations.

You'll want to ask for—and check—references, taking care to ask how long each reference has been with the RSO, what their experiences have been, and approximately how many guests they get from the agency each season. Make copies of the "RSO Evaluation" below and use them when you interview your prospects.

RSO Evaluation

1. What advertising and marketing do you do? _____

_____

(Ask to see copies of brochures, newsletters, magazine ads, etc., as well as any magazine or other press clippings.)

2. Do you have a web site? What's the address? _____

_____

(Get on the web and check out the site for yourself. Does it look professional and inviting? How easy is it to navigate? Does it give a description of each B&B? Are there photos of each?)

3. Do you actively market each B&B on your books? _____

4. Is it easy for prospective guests to make reservations or ask questions? How often is e-mail answered, and what are your telephone business hours? _____

_____

5. Do you work with travel agents? _____

6. How often are host listings updated? _____

7. Do you belong to Bed & Breakfast Reservation Services Worldwide or The National Network? _____

8. Do you perform home inspections? _____

RSO Evaluation, continued

9. After the initial inspection, how often (if at all) do you do check-ups? __

   _____

10. Do you ask guests for evaluations? Do you pass the information on to hosts? _____

   _____

11. Do you confirm reservations with hosts before booking? _____

12. Do you make recommendations on setting room rates? _____

13. Do you take deposits from guests? What is your deposit policy? _____

   _____

14. What is your cancellation policy? _____

   _____

15. How knowledgeable are you about state and local regulations that pertain to B&Bs? _____

   _____

16. Do you sponsor events and education for hosts? _____

17. What, if any, group discounts do you offer, such as liability insurance or purchasing plans for linens, towels, or housekeeping products? _____

   _____

18. Please provide me with a list of references.

   _____

   _____

   _____

   _____

   _____

   (Don't forget to check these out!)

Apple PAII

While the reservation service can be a tremendous boost to your knowledge base and your earnings, you may choose not to go with one. Bill and Sandra Wayne, who run a historic farmhouse B&B in southwestern Missouri, used an RSO to give their inn a kick-start but have since dropped it. "It was worthwhile back when we started," Bill says, "but times have changed." The inn's own web site and various online B&B guides now provide plenty of reservations.

Even if you don't use an RSO, you'll want to belong to something. Professional associations provide the same education, information, and support as the RSO—and you don't have to give them commissions.

Perhaps the flagship of innkeeping organizations is the Professional Association of Innkeepers International, otherwise known as PAII (remember, it's pronounced like "pie"). Founded in 1988 by two innkeepers who've professionally been there and done it all, PAII offers a bevy of reasons to join, including:

- a free listing for your B&B on the association's web site, www.innplace.com
- discounts on books (and there are lots of innkeeping texts on offer), conferences, advertising, credit card merchant fees, and other vendor services
- discounts on vendor products and services
- discounts on the rates banks charge when you take guests' credit card payments
- personal consultation on your promotional ideas
- a subscription to the association's monthly journal, *Innkeeping*
- a free members-only HOT-PAII help line, where professional assistance is available 24/7

New Jersey-based PAII also gives members a voice in the hospitality and travel industries through its contacts with organizations such as the American Hotel and Motel Association, the Automobile Association of America, the Travel Industry Association and the National Restaurant Association. The cost for all this is $175 per year.

Help yourself to another piece of pie and check out local associations. Most states and many regional areas have their own B&B associations. Member perks, of course, vary with the organization but are generally well worth the membership fee. Bonuses typically include a listing on the association's web site, marketing activities, newsletters, and support from staff and other members.

Another very important asset is quality assurance. Most associations are self-regulating and send out staff to inspect each of their member properties annually. As a result, guests feel more secure in booking a room with a clean, safe, and attractive inn, which in turn means more revenues for hosts.

But it also means that membership fees for state and regional B&B associations can be higher than those in other industries. Annual dues range from $50 per property to $225 per property with an additional $5 per room to $25 per room.

Restore America

You know all the benefits of the bed and breakfast—romance, friendliness, and a safe and cozy home-away-from-home atmosphere. Your guests either already know or are eager to discover the B&B experience. But you may find people out there who don't know these things and, like Queen Victoria at her most uppity, are not amused by the idea of a B&B in their neighborhood. And they can tend to put a few bumps in your road to success. Not to worry. They can usually be mollified with a little education on the benefits of bed and breakfasts in their communities.

The truth is that B&Bs are stabilizing as well as income-producing influences (not just for the owner but for the town). Take at look at these benefits:

- *Neighborhood renovation and revitalization.* As many as 90 percent of bed and breakfasts occupy historic buildings that have been lovingly restored and returned to active life. Without B&Bs, most of these grand old dames would be neighborhood eyesores, beacons for rats and vandals, or bits of scattered rubble at the county landfill or architectural salvage yard. As B&Bs, they help bring new spirit and energy to the neighborhood, often in the vanguard of new shops and eateries—in short, a healthy new economy. A recent PAII/YBR Marketing report revealed that $1 billion in private funds had been spent annually to restore and preserve historic properties used as inns or B&Bs. YBR, or Yellow Brick Road, is a Julian, California, company that produces a newsletter for aspiring innkeepers.

- *Economic input.* B&Bs also contribute to the economy by bringing in tourist dollars. And tourists spend a lot. Not only do they pay the innkeeper money that's then circulated in the local economy, but they dine out, pay for admission to local attractions, and buy souvenirs, clothing, gifts, sundries, and gasoline. According to a recent survey by PAII and YBR Marketing, the average guest couple (and most guests are couples) spends more than $225 per day on lodging, food, and incidentals.

> **Fun Fact**
> What is the favorite activity of U.S. travelers? Shopping, says the Travel Industry Association of America. Shopaholics stay an average of 4.2 nights at a given destination and spend about $531 per trip—and that doesn't include the cost of transportation.

- *Historic preservation.* B&B owners are the guardians of community history. Since they restore instead of revamp their aged treasures, often furnishing them with period antiques, they create living museums. In addition, bed and breakfast innkeepers tend to collect old photos, letters, and other local memorabilia to display and share.

- *Neighborhood watch.* Because the innkeepers are at home during the day instead of

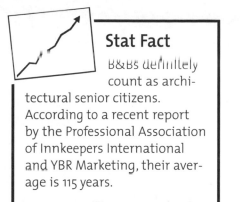

Stat Fact

B&Bs definitely count as architectural senior citizens. According to a recent report by the Professional Association of Innkeepers International and YBR Marketing, their average is 115 years.

away at the office for eight to ten hours at a stretch, they help ensure neighborhood safety. Neighbors often worry—especially in the case of potential homestays that will operate in strictly residential areas—that the street will fall prey to roving bands of burglarizing strangers. But with reservation services and the hosts themselves to screen guests, this is not a problem. Also, most B&B guests are affluent, upper-income types who aren't into a stretch in the slammer for the instant gratification of pilfering a car radio or a bike. Industry experts report that theft among B&B guests is so low as to be virtually nonexistent.

3

Dreaming On
Market Research

There's a lot more to transforming your dream of a B&B into a reality than just choosing designer towels for the bathrooms. First comes replacing fantasy with the hard-core planning stage. Just like every home—whether it is a Queen Anne mansion or contemporary ranch—is carefully designed, with architectural elevations, blueprints, and floor plans, every B&B needs to undergo the same careful planning. Instead of researching building and zoning codes and pouring over plumbing and electrical schematics, however, you'll research the type of guests you can attract and plan how you'll woo them. In other words, you'll want to conduct market research.

This is an extremely important part of any new business start-up. The more facts and figures at your fingertips, the more information you reap. Market research helps you determine if there are enough potential guests in your region for the type of B&B you have in mind, as well as whether those guests will want to stay with you.

Business or Pleasure

First you'll want to decide on one or more target markets. Aside from the rare bank robber on the lam, travelers typically fall into specific categories such as vacation and business, to name just two. If your B&B will be located in an area with no tourist attractions, you may have a hard time attracting the former; if you set up in a locale with no industry, you're unlikely to attract the latter. You should carefully consider what will bring travelers in and who they'll be.

Nancy Helsper in San Diego attributes her inn's covetous 80 percent year-round occupancy to both her location and her market strategy. Located in an area that's rich in tourist attractions and that's also an urban metropolis, she's able to target the leisure tourist and the business traveler. And with her storybook Victorian mansion , she's also able to attract a sizable wedding market. "That and the corporate market made us," Nancy says.

Take a look at the following typical target markets. If you can pull in two, or several, that's great. But you'll need to attract at least one—or get creative and come up with something else that will bring in ample visitors.

- *Tourists*. The quintessential vacationers, these are the people who're out for a good time. Visiting amusement parks, national parks, museums, beach-combing, boating, skiing, sightseeing, and, of course, shopping are their modus operandi. If you're close to any sort of natural or man-made attraction that brings people in, you've got a great market. The tourist market can be extremely seasonal—summertime for sun worshippers and winter for skiers—and in between, sporadic weekends throughout the year, depending on your location. In

Fun Fact

Romance isn't cheap—at least not while the wedding ceremony is still fresh. Honeymooners spend over three times more than the average traveler, according to the Travel Industry Association of America.

metropolitan beacons like Manhattan and Los Angeles, for instance, you'll find a more stable market because people come for the city attractions rather than romping in the surf or snow. Your location, however, may have a different high season altogether. In New England, for instance, the leaf peepers turn out en masse to view the fall colors and stay at country inns and B&Bs.

- *Business travelers.* Whether traveling salespeople or company presidents, business trippers account for a lot of lodging stays. At most recent count, says the Travel Industry Association of America (TIA), 210.5 million business trips were taken in a single year, and more and more business travelers are opting for the joys of the B&B over the impersonality of a hotel. As a trendy example, Oprah Winfrey chose a bed and breakfast while ensconced in Amarillo, Texas, for her landmark court battle against the cattle barons. If you'll be in an urban locale, business travelers could be a terrific market for you. But you don't have to be based in New York City or Chicago to attract the commercial trade. Many small towns and suburbs boast one or two large corporations that generate a lot of income—and a fair amount of business travel. As an added bonus, business travel, unlike the tourist trade, isn't seasonal.

- *Romance.* Everyone loves a romantic getaway, and the bed and breakfast is its epitome, so this market is terrific for many a B&B. It's a sizable one—nearly 42 million Americans, or 20 percent of all adults, splurged on a romantic weekend or longer in a recently surveyed year, says the TIA. The average traveler, it adds, revved up with two-and-a-half romantic trips during the same year. "Our cottage is designed for romantic getaways," Bill and Sandra Wayne in Missouri say, "and is heavy on anniversaries."

- *College or university.* If you're located in a college town, close to the siss-boom-bah of the cheerleaders and marching band, you've got a built-in market, at least during certain times of the year. Football games, homecomings, and graduations, not to mention new student orientations and parents' weekends, conferences, and other academic or public events, can bring visitors in droves. And since many college towns are also small towns with little lodging competition, this market could be yours in which to shine. Keep in mind that your business will be seasonal unless you an augment it with another target market.

- *Hospital.* Sickness may equal fiduciary health for you if your B&B is located near a major medical center. People can find themselves spending days, weeks, or months away from home to stay at the bedsides of ill loved ones. And while this is an ordeal you wouldn't wish on anyone, it feels good to be able to offer them a room in your home instead of in a cold and indifferent hotel. Hospitals can also draw a number of business travelers in the form of visiting physicians, lecturers, and conference attendees—who can be a terrific market for you.

- *Locals' extra bedroom*. You might think people who already live in your town wouldn't be interested in your B&B. But you can develop a tidy additional market by promoting yourself to locals as "your extra bedrooms." Somebody is always having a wedding, family reunion, or other event for which they invite lots of out-of-town visitors . . . and then have nowhere to put them up. You can fill the gap.

> **Fun Fact**
> Baby boomers generated the highest travel volume in the United States in 2003, registering 268.9 million trips. (Domestic Travel Market Report, 2004)

- *Town society spot*. Many B&Bs, especially those in small towns, position themselves as the place for local clubs and organizations to hold teas, meetings, and other get-togethers. After all, what makes a more charming site for a book club meeting, chamber of commerce function, or garden club tea than the drawing room or parlor of the local historic home? This business is unlikely to garner you overnight guests (unless guest speakers are involved), but it can be a welcome supplement to your income and promote your establishment to locals to remember when recommending accommodations to out-of-town friends.

Specialty of the House

As you target your market, start thinking "market niche." This is the specialty of the house that makes your bed and breakfast stand out from the crowd and the competition. It might be the wedding gazebo in the garden, the library in the turret, or the toy chest in the den.

Your niche might be one of the following:

- *Historic*. Many B&Bs are in historic buildings; if yours will be one of them, you can capitalize on your bit of the past. Develop a niche by offering guests an authentic taste of the Old South, for example, or a Victorian Christmas, or life on a turn-of-the-20th-century farm. You'll want to combine all this, of course, with 21st century amenities, but you carry out your theme with authentic furnishings and memorabilia.

- *Health, beauty, and fitness*. You might develop a niche as a heart-healthy B&B that serves gourmet vegetarian dishes or organically grown goodies. You could cater to fitness-crazed guests with an exercise room or mountain bikes. Or how about an in-room day spa with an on-call massage therapist or beauty consultant for facials and nails? If you're not qualified, local experts will be delighted to make arrangements with you.

- *Weddings and romance*. Like David and Marilyn Lewis in Fort Worth, Texas, you might make romance your niche. They offer the garden for weddings (and even David's services as a minister) and go all-out with a romantic theme of heart-shaped whirlpool tubs, heart-shaped cookies, cupids and cherubs, romance-themed art, and romantic books and letters scattered throughout their cottages. "We want it to be a memory, a wonderful place,"Marilyn says.

> **Smart Tip** Tip...
>
> Make your market cele brations, like Bruce and Judy Albert in Seaside, Florida, who say, "Our guests have been event travelers—[those visiting for] honeymoons, anniversaries, birthdays, and college graduations."

- *Kid-proof*. Most B&Bs don't welcome children. If you love kids, you can offer traveling families the bed-and-breakfast experience. You might try child-proof quarters, chests packed with toys in a special nursery, cribs, or youth beds, or even an old-fashioned sleeping porch for those balmy summer nights. You could even offer babysitting services (yourself or contracted out) so parents can have a night on the town. While their cottage is geared toward romantic twosomes, the Waynes in Missouri also target families with their farmhouse suite.

- *Lessons or workshops*. If you're a master crafter, artist, cook, or gardener, you can carve out a niche by offering lessons in your specialty. Americans love to learn

Destination Known

If you've got a location that's off the beaten track, with no tourist attractions, no industry, and no college or other institutions to draw visitors, you may still be able to pull in a market. Develop your B&B as a destination in itself.

Some innkeepers offer their properties as visits at working farms or cattle ranches. You may be able to develop yours as a deluxe fish camp or canoe station, if you're on a lake or stream; a hunting lodge in duck or deer country; an equestrian's paradise with riding trails amid stunning scenery; or a gold mining or gem-hunting resort out in the desert.

An option like this will, of course, require a lot more marketing and promotion than the B&B that's down the street from Disneyland or in a famous seaside resort. But it can be done. Just use your imagination!

while vacationing. One-fifth of U.S. travelers (that's 30.2 million adults) have taken a trip specifically to learn or improve a skill, sport, or hobby in the last three years of a recent survey, says the TIA.

- *Special interest groups*. If you belong to a special interest group—anything from birdwatchers to Civil War buffs—and your locale will interest your members, you can cultivate a niche just for them. Besides your own local advice and trip tips, you could boast an interest-rich library of books on your subject for browsing, as well as maps, charts, and artwork.

- *Haunted history*. If your historic home boasts a ghost or two in the attic, you might develop this as your niche. You'll have to make sure your ghosts are friendly and that you tantalize guests rather than spook them to the point where they won't stay.

Will They Come?

By this point you may have realized that where you locate your B&B and its success are closely intertwined. Whether you plan to convert your present home into a bed and breakfast or are going to go out and buy a property, you'll need to consider your locale and whether it will attract visitors. Just because you convert, renovate, or build it doesn't mean they will come. With lots of imagination and promotion, you may be able to create a market, but you'll be far better off if you choose an area that has a strong customer base.

"You need to look at where you'll buy your property," advises innkeeper Nancy Helsper in San Diego. "A lady recently told me she was very excited because she was going to build an inn in a town with no hotels. Hotels are very astute—this means there's no business. People don't realize that romantic weekend getaways alone are not going to provide an income.

"Sacramento, California, a state capitol, is big on business travel," Nancy continues. "Innkeepers there can charge double what I do on weekdays but can't get anything on weekends. Who says, 'Honey, let's go to Sacramento for the weekend?' Innkeepers in Julian, a small, resort town in the mountains east of San Diego, get only weekend business. Nobody says, 'Let's go to Julian on Tuesday night.'"

This is not to say you should delete resort areas from your wish list, just that you need to

> **Tip...**
>
> ## Smart Tip
> "Visit as many B&Bs as you can," innkeeper Nancy S. in Bayfield, Wisconsin, advises. "Keep a notebook of what you like and what you don't. Start visualizing and dreaming what your place will be."

factor in your financial needs as well as your emotional wants. "Look at the income you need," Nancy counsels. "You could have a 40 percent occupancy and be happy if you had no debt service."

Nancy and Steve Sandstrom have made a thriving success of their B&B in the small destination resort town of Bayfield, Wisconsin. They boast full occupancy June 15 through October 15, and also target guests all through the winter months by offering complimentary snowshoes and promoting winter sports from dog-sledding to skiing. "We tell people this is a fantastic place for winter," Nancy says. "The best way to survive winter is to get out and play in it. Don't hole up inside."

Whether you have in mind sled dogs or surfboards, an important part of your market research will be to determine if the area you have your heart set on meets visitor criteria. Use the "Location Research Worksheet" on page 38 to help define the best area for your B&B. Make several copies and fill out one for each of your potential locations.

Where do you get the answers to all these questions? You've got a variety of sources to query. Start with the following:

- *Local chambers of commerce and downtown improvement boards.* These exist for the purpose of attracting new business; they should be able to provide you with a wealth of information. If they don't have the information you need, ask for suggestions on where to find it.

- *Local tourism or convention and visitors bureaus.* These people know what type of visitors come into town, at what times of the year, and how long they stay per visit. They can tell you what festivals, fairs, conventions, and other events are held seasonally, and how many visitors they attract. They should also be able to tell you what types of lodging are the most popular and what their rates are.

- *Local commercial real estate agents.* These folks know the area and should be able to give you the dirt on local lodgings, industry, and the economy.

- *Local newspapers.* Peruse the ads and calendar of events. What's going on in town that will attract visitors? What sort of restaurants and lodgings have ads running? What are their prices?

- *Local Yellow Pages.* Look under "Hotels" and "Bed & Breakfasts." How many are listed? What do their ads look like?

- *Shop around.* Be a looky-loo—pop into hotels, motels, and B&Bs and see what they look like. Prosperous or dismal? Collect brochures and rate sheets. Ask about off-season dates and rates.

Ask lots of questions. Become a collector; glom onto any brochures, rate sheets, mailers, or other advertising information, all of which will help you form a picture of towns with potential.

Location Research Worksheet

1. What is the area population? _____

2. Is there significant business and industry in the area? _____

3. Are there any of the following in the area to bring in visitors:

   • Major medical center _____

   • Center of government _____

   • College or university _____

   • Major employer _____

4. Is the area a popular vacation destination? _____

5. Where do most tourist visitors in the area come from? _____

6. Is the location within three hours of one or more metropolitan areas? __

   _____

7. Or is it in a metropolitan area itself? _____

8. What will encourage visitors to spend one or more nights?

   • Beaches _____

   • Fishing _____

   • Boating _____

   • Rafting or canoeing _____

   • Skiing _____

   • Shopping _____

   • Restaurants _____

   • Amusement parks _____

   • Museums _____

   • Gardens _____

   • Other cultural attractions _____

   • Historical sights _____

   • Scenery _____

   • Special events (festivals, fairs, sporting events, etc.) _____

9. Are the area's attractions seasonal? _____

10. If so, what is the high season? _____

Location Research Worksheet, continued

11. Is there a viable off-season or does everything close down (like in *The Shining*)? _____

12. How do visitors reach the area (plane, car, train)? _____

13. Are there convenient highways, airports, or train stations to serve them? _____

14. How long does the average visitor spend in the area? _____

    _____

15. How many lodging facilities are in the area?
    - Hotels _____
    - Motels _____
    - Inns _____
    - B&Bs _____

16. How many new lodging facilities have opened in the past two years? ___

    _____

17. How many have gone out of business in the past two years and why?

    _____

18. What are high season and low season rates for hotels, motels, inns, and B&Bs in the area? _____

    _____

    (If rates are similarly high year-round, business is good; if they're similarly low year-round, the lodging business in the area is not doing well. A drastic difference between high and low seasons is indicative of fierce competition and/or a major seasonal lull.)

19. Are minimum stays required at local lodgings? _____

20. If so, all year or for which times of the year? _____

21. Do local lodgings offer midweek stay or other discounts? _____

22. What are occupancy rates for hotels, motels, inns, and B&Bs in the area?

    _____

    (Don't count lodgings with conference facilities as these will skew the figures.)

Location Research Worksheet, continued

23. What amenities do local B&Bs offer (e.g., fireplace, whirlpool tub, swimming pool, croquet lawn, evening snacks, suites)? _____

_____

24. How do prices vary with offered amenities? _____

25. How involved and aware are the chamber of commerce, tourism or visitors bureau, and other government agencies in supporting tourism and lodging? _____

_____

26. What is the state of the local economy? _____

27. Are there any economic or tourism red flags such as closure of factories or other industry in the local area or within the radius from which your clientele will come? _____

_____

_____

28. Is there any land change usage on the horizon that would impact tourism (e.g., closing parkland to skiers or hunters, limiting number of visitors to scenic areas)? _____

_____

Healthy Competition

While you're conducting all this market research, don't forget to check out the competition. Depending on your location, your rivals may be hotels, motels, country inns, full-scale resorts, and other B&Bs. This is not a bad thing; a little competition is healthy. If there are a number of lodgings in your area and they're all doing well, chances are you will, too. It means business is good.

"Our market research told us there weren't that many bed and breakfasts in Fort Worth," David Lewis says. "The ones available had only three to four rooms. There were a few more inns in outlying areas. But ours is a great location because it's near the cultural district and Will Rogers Coliseum, and people come from out of town [to be guests] at my studios."

"And lots of people come to bed and breakfasts instead of hotels for the charm," Marilyn adds. "And this house has a lot of charm and history."

Like David and Marilyn, you'll need to consider what will draw guests to you instead of your competitors. Start by considering these factors:

- What is your competition doing that works?
- What can you successfully copy?
- What are they doing that you can do better?
- What can you offer that will draw customers away from them and to you? You can answer these questions by performing the following research tasks:
  - Surf B&B reservation service and association web sites, which are packed with listings—complete with photos—of all sorts of bed and breakfasts all over the country and the globe. Study what others are doing and explore what sounds good to you, what doesn't, and what you'd like to emulate, expand on, or change.
  - Take some trips. Visit as many B&Bs as you can as a guest. Observe what other bed and breakfasts look like, how they work, and what they offer.
  - Pore over bed and breakfast guides, which you can buy at your local bookseller or online through sources like Amazon.com and Barnes & Noble.
  - Send for B&B brochures and observe, once again, what's on offer, what sounds good, what doesn't, and why.

Statistics Central

Collecting information about potential locations is incredibly important. But garnering information—good old hard-core statistics—is also an important market research tool, especially if you'll approach a bank or other lender for start-up capital. You'll want facts and figures on the B&B, lodging, and travel industries. And if you'll target a particular market, like newlyweds, young families, birdwatchers, or hunters, you'll want to know how many of them there are and where.

These types of figures will help you determine just how many prospective customers you can expect and if that number is large enough to be lucrative. Where do you get all this statistical stuff?

Go public—library that is. Ask your local reference librarian. Pay him a visit and explain

Stat Fact
The top three states that serve as destinations to the domestic and international traveler, according to the Travel Industry Association of America, are California, Florida, and Texas.

what you need to know and why. Tell him you need to know how many weddings there were in the United States at last count, the number of Audubon Society members in the Southwest, how many hunters in Texas or families with children under 12 in the United States. He'll put all sorts of stats at your fingertips.

Go to the web. You'll find all sorts of information on the internet. Start with the United States Census Bureau, then try web sites of specific organizations, from associations of wedding planners to the Audubon Society to the National Rifle Association. And don't forget the phone. If you can't find the information you want on the net, call the associations themselves and ask.

Go to B&B lodging and travel industry sources, especially ones like PAII and local B&B reservation services—you'll find contact information in the Appendix at the back of this book. They're out there to help you and will be particularly helpful if you're already a member. It's smart to join!

Mail Mania

If you'll target a particular market, like those birdwatchers, crafters, gardeners, Civil War buffs or young families, you can check the size and interest level of your target market through direct-mail surveys. To do this, you send questionnaires to the people you believe will make up your ideal market and ask them their travel and lodging preferences and habits.

If you belong to an association, organization, or listserv (e-mail mailing list) that happens to be affiliated with your target market (like the Audubon Society, Garden Club of Georgia, or Mothers of Twins), you're in luck. You may already have a directory packed with names, addresses, and even phone numbers at your fingertips. If not, you may be able to beg, borrow, or buy a directory from the organization's main office. You can also buy batches of names from list brokers who specialize in supplying lists for just about every interest group in existence. Prices run about $50 per 1,000 names. (For more on this, read Chapter 11.)

> **Tip...**
>
> **Smart Tip**
> People are unlikely to return a mail survey unless you offer them an incentive. How about a coupon for 10 percent off their first stay at your B&B? This gives you a head start on bookings and also helps spread the word about you—and word-of-mouth sells.

What should you ask? Check out the "Direct-Mail Survey" on page 43. Your queries will relate to your own target market and B&B location, but you can use this as a starting point for what and how to ask.

Gull Cottage Bed & Breakfast

A Seaside Cottage Out of Time

How would you like to be able to take time out from today's hectic world and spend time enjoying the simple things in life: the sound and rhythm of the sea, the silky feel of the breeze on your skin, and the scent of roses and sea air?

Sound too wonderful to be true? Not so! Gull Cottage Bed & Breakfast is only a few hours' drive from home—the perfect spot to relax and unwind for a three-day getaway or a three-week vacation. Be transported to a quiet, rejuvenating world where there's always plenty of time. (If you're lucky, you may even catch a glimpse of our former owner—always considered a sign of good fortune by our guests.) To encourage you to visit Gull Cottage, I'd like to offer you a special gift.

But first, I need your help. To tailor the inn to your needs and desires, I'm asking you to fill out the enclosed questionnaire and send it back. It's a self-mailer, so it's easy! To show my appreciation, once I've received your answers, I'll send you a coupon for 10 percent off any three-night or longer stay within the next six months.

- Fill out the questionnaire.

- Send it back.

- And get ready to relax and unwind here on our timeless shore.

Magically yours,

Caroline Muir

000 Turtle Lane,
Sullivan's Island, SC 00000
(000) 000-0000
www.gullcottagebb.com

Direct-Mail Survey, continued

Gull Cottage
Help Us Design the Perfect
Bed & Breakfast for You

1. Do you travel on business? _____

2. If so, how often? _____

3. Where do you travel on business? _____

   _____

4. During what times of the year? _____

5. For how long? _____

6. Where do you normally stay (hotel, motel, B&B)? _____

7. How long do you usually stay in one lodging facility while away from home? _____

8. How much do you usually spend per night on lodging? _____

9. Do you travel for pleasure? _____

10. If so, how often? _____

11. Where do you travel for pleasure? _____

    _____

12. During what times of the year? _____

13. For how long? _____

14. Where do you normally stay (hotel, motel, B&B, campground, etc.)? _____

    _____

15. How long do you usually stay in one lodging facility while away from home? _____

16. How much do you usually spend per night on lodging? _____

17. Have you ever stayed in a bed and breakfast? _____

18. If so, please tell me what you most enjoyed about your stay. _____

    _____

Direct-Mail Survey, continued

19. Was any part of your stay unappealing? _____

_____

20. Please rate the following amenities in order of which is most appealing to you, with 1 being the most important and 20 the least:

__ King-sized bed
__ Fireplace
__ Whirlpool tub
__ Balcony
__ View
__ Sitting room off bedroom
__ TV
__ VCR
__ CD player
__ Computer with games
__ Computer with internet access and fax

__ Minibar
__ Antiques
__ Library stocked with books
__ Video library
__ Gas grill/barbecue
__ Private kitchen
__ Private dining area
__ Private bath
__ Swimming pool

21. Do you usually travel alone or with others? _____

22. If with others, who are they (spouse, children, friends, business associates)?

_____

23. Please rate the following activities in order of which is most appealing to you, with 1 being the most important and 12 the least:

__ Sightseeing
__ Shopping
__ Relaxing
__ Swimming
__ Boating
__ Fishing
__ Golfing

__ Beachcombing
__ Sunbathing
__ Cultural activities (historic houses, museums, theater)
__ Amusement parks
__ Dining

Focal Points

If you plan to use your present location and garner business from locals—as a destination for wedding guest overflow, garden society teas, or whatever—then take advantage of another way to conduct market research: the focus group. Here you invite anywhere from 5 to 12 people into your living room and pepper them with questions. Of course, you don't pull in any old body—just as with other forms of market research, you choose your respondents with care. You might invite, for instance, members of the local chamber of commerce, the book or garden club, or individuals you know who have a finger on the pulse of the area and might provide you with business.

Once you've assembled your group—or groups if you plan to hold more than one focus session—you should offer them some sort of refreshment (which will show off your hosting and culinary skills), and hand out your questionnaires along with pencils for filling them in. Take a look at the "Focus Group Questionnaire" below and then formulate your own based on your area and target market. Ask as many questions as you feel your group can handle and encourage discussion. You'll learn a lot!

Stat Fact

People who travel to experience culture and history spend more money, stay in hotels more often, visit more destinations, and are doubly likely to take a trip for entertainment than any other travelers, says the Travel Industry Association of America.

Focus Group Questionnaire

1. How many times a year do you have out-of-town guests who spend at least one night? _____

2. For what sorts of occasions do your guests visit? _____
_____

3. Who are your most frequent out-of-town guests (e.g., siblings, friends, grown children with families, elderly parents, business associates)? _____
_____

4. Where do they usually stay? _____

5. How long do they stay per visit? _____

6. If at a hotel, motel, or inn, do you make the reservations for your guests?
_____

7. If so, how much is usually spent on a room per night? _____

8. Are you planning an event (wedding, anniversary, graduation, or other) within the next year that will bring in friends and relatives from out of town?

_____

_____

9. Do you like the idea of housing your guests at a local bed and breakfast?

_____

10. Would you make reservations for them at one? _____

11. What would you expect room rates at a bed and breakfast to be? _____

_____

12. Which local clubs, groups, or associations do you belong to? _____

_____

13. Would your group or association be interested in holding meetings or special events (afternoon teas, board meetings, officer investitures, or other) in a charmingly appointed bed and breakfast drawing room or parlor?

_____

14. What would your group expect to spend for a two-hour event that would include coffee, tea, and scones or similar refreshments? _____

_____

15. What would your group expect to spend for a four-hour afternoon with the same refreshments? _____

16. Please comment on the name Gull Cottage Bed & Breakfast (love, like, dislike, or hate and why). _____

_____

17. Please comment on the name Mermaid Lane Bed & Breakfast (love, like, dislike, or hate and why). _____

_____

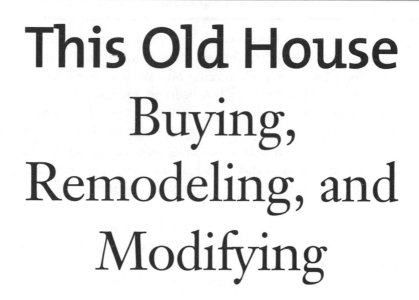

This Old House

Buying, Remodeling, and Modifying

Y ou can't have a bed and breakfast without a house to have the beds and breakfasts in. So one of your most important start-up tasks will be getting your residence up and running. This can mean buying a house or other building and renovating it, modifying your present home for B&B use, purchasing an existing B&B, or building a brand-new structure. In this chapter, we'll explore all these options and more, as we burrow into building department bureaucracy, zip up the zoning issue, and basically help you nail down that dream B&B.

The Old Homestead

Perhaps the easiest option is to stay put—to use your present home as a B&B. Whether or not you'll do so will depend on a lot of factors, not the least of which are the size of your house and how much income you want to earn: the fewer bedrooms, the lower your earnings. If you've got a two-bedroom townhouse or a four-bedroom bungalow (and one bedroom in either one is yours), and you'll be happy with a supplemental income, then you can consider using your current digs.

If you've got a sprawling farmhouse or family mansion with plenty of bedrooms not currently in use and a mom-in-law cottage in the back, or if you've inherited your grandparents' 1950s Florida motel, then you're on the right track for more than supplemental revenues.

But stay tuned—bathrooms are also a big issue. When B&Bs first started up in this country, shared baths were perfectly acceptable. They were part of the B&B experience. Today, however, with more sophisticated guests, more luxurious bed and breakfasts to choose from, and rampaging germs getting constant media coverage, shared baths are not cool.

Park It . . . But Where?

While you're standing in the street gazing at your house, consider the matter of parking. Is there adequate off-street space for your family vehicles plus one for each guest room? If you don't have a huge driveway or parking pad, can you put a guest car or two on the street—any day or night of the week?

Some neighborhoods have stringent resident-only requirements, and some require that cars be moved once a week for street cleaning. Your guests won't appreciate having to get up at 5 A.M. to drive their cars to the other side of the street. Then there are the neighbors, who may pitch fits over the idea of strangers' vehicles cluttering up their street at all hours. These are all issues you need to address before opening your doors to guests.

This is not to say you absolutely can't have guest rooms with shared baths—a number of B&Bs and homestays still offer them. But if you go this route, you'll lose a lot of business from potential guests who'll pass you by. The Professional Association of Innkeepers International says that private baths are basic. "If you don't believe it, you'll learn it your first year. Occupancy with a shared bath is much lower, unless you're marketing to a much lower income population.

The trend is toward luxury and the upscale side. B&Bs used to be entry level, in the $35 to $55 per night range." Today rooms can mount into the $300 to $400 per night range for a very special stay.

So again, you'll need to think about why you're going into the business. If it's for the joys of meeting people combined with the perks of a little extra income, then you may choose to go ahead with shared baths. If not, you'll have to go house-hunting. (Or add on a bath or two.)

Curb Appeal and Character

Your home's curb appeal and character are two more issues to consider, and again, you'll have to think about who you'll target as your market. If your guests' main reasons for staying with you will be your budget pricing and proximity to local sights or institutions, then you may do fine with an average, unassuming tract house. Keep in mind, however, that you won't get top room rates.

If you plan to go after tourists or business travelers in search of luxury accommodations and a romantic B&B experience, you'll need a house that meets their expectations. It doesn't necessarily have to be a Victorian mansion bristling with towers, turrets, and gingerbread. It can be an old-fashioned ranch house, a contemporary log cabin or a sleek chrome-and-glass studio—what matters is that it offers guests a unique experience due to its history, architecture, or location, or some combination thereof, that they don't have at home and won't find at a hotel or motel.

Step outside yourself for a moment and scrutinize your home with a stranger's point of view. What do you see? Does your house have curb appeal? Would someone driving up for the first time be enchanted with the landscaping or dismayed by overgrown shrubbery, an unkempt lawn, or a barren plot? What about the house itself? Is it cheerful and well-maintained or in need of paint, new screens, and general maintenance?

Bed and breakfast homes need to be not only tidy but inviting. Yours should have an easily navigable walkway and adequate night lighting so guests arriving after dark feel safe and welcome. Rockers on the porch, a wreath on the door, and potted plants on the steps all contribute to a cheerful ambience.

Your home may be the best one on the block, but if the block is rundown or unsafe, you'll have a hard time garnering guests. So while you're giving your house the fine-tooth comb treatment, do the same with your neighborhood. It doesn't have to be Beverly Hills' Rodeo Drive, but like your home, it should be clean, well-maintained, and inviting.

Personal Space

Next you'll need to consider the privacy issue. Every innkeeper, no matter how much of a "people person," needs personal space. And the larger your family, the more space you'll need. While a singleton might be content with a separate suite containing bedroom and bath, a boisterous family will need room for parents and kids to spread out, make noise, and get messy. You may think this isn't an issue, but think again. Sooner or later it will be, and the wise course is to address it now.

"The innkeeper lives in the pits—the least desirable room," laughs Nancy Sandstrom in Wisconsin. "We converted the old summer kitchen into our two-story living quarters. It's the smallest space we've lived in since we've been married. But it's behind the kitchen and we're able to close the door, which is good for the guests and good for us."

"You really need personal space," Nancy Helsper in San Diego agrees. "You can't live in the room that's not rented. You need to have a place that's your own. You have to take care of the caregiver."

Ideally, you should have completely separate quarters from your guests, either in a cottage or carriage house away from the main building or in a separate wing of the house. If you can't have one of these, try for as much privacy as possible. Many innkeepers suggest that you choose a bedroom that doesn't share a common wall with guest rooms. You should have your own living room, which could be your former den or family room, and, of course, you'll need your very own bathroom, one that's ideally in your bedroom so you don't have to dart out into a common hallway to use it.

Remodeler's Revenge

What if your neighborhood is a sightseers' dream, your house oozes charm, has plenty of bedrooms and adequate parking, but there's no place to call your own? Are there only two bathrooms for five bedrooms?

Remodel—with a plan. Before you decide to take over half the garden with a new master suite, for instance, look at how you may be able to use space you already have. Can you convert a walk-in closet to a bathroom? This is not as drastic as it might sound. B&B guests don't

Smart Tip
"Some innkeepers mark the doors to their personal quarters 'Laundry' or 'Storage' so guests can't figure out where they disappeared to," offers innkeeper Nancy Helsper in San Diego.

Yours, Mine, and Ours?

Would-be homestay hosts often make the mistake of thinking they can shunt B&B guests into Junior's bedroom now that he's away at school without making any changes to the decor. This doesn't work. This is not a yours-mine-and-ours situation. Guests will not be impressed with the football and rock star posters on the walls, glow-in-the-dark stars on the ceiling, and race car circuit stickers on the windows. They won't like having to share closet space with the gear and clothing Junior didn't cart off to college.

Guests are also uncomfortable in bedrooms where your family photos are displayed on dressers, tables, and nightstands, and in gathering rooms that are festooned with your bowling trophies and Little League awards. And, of course, you should never, ever leave personal toiletries and medications in bathrooms that will be used by guests.

You're aiming to make guests feel at home, but not as if they've intruded into your home. Pack the personal mementos into your private quarters, and leave the historical, whimsical, or elegant ones for your guests.

need storage space for out-of-season clothes, out-of-style shoes that are bound to be back in style someday, party dresses that were worn once, golf clubs, bowling balls, and grandma's luggage collection. They'll actually be happier with a period-piece armoire that has more than enough room for what they've brought along.

Look at your residence with a new eye. Perhaps there's a bedroom sandwiched between two other bedrooms that could be partitioned down the middle and turned into two private baths, one for each bedroom. True, you'll lose a bedroom, but the two private baths will more than make up the income potential of the lost bedroom.

Remodeling, of course, is a major undertaking that can be either exciting or nightmarish, depending on you, your contractor, and your checkbook. To enjoy the process, you must have a healthy imagination, a belief in happy endings, and a disposition cheerful enough to withstand noise, dirt, drywall dust, and workmen tromping through your home from 7 A.M. to dusk for weeks or even months on end. And any contractor or designer will tell you to budget upfront for unexpected cost overruns.

Picture Pretty

When your home is a bed and breakfast, you're living in a set designed not for a movie audience but for the benefit of your guests. Furnishings and decor must work together to carry out a theme, whether it be Laura Ashley Country, Victorian, or nattily nautical. So if your house was last decorated when your college-age kids were infants, it might be time to change that flocked wallpaper and mowable shag carpet.

Examine your furnishings the same way you did your home's exterior. Are they shabby chic or just shabby? Are there places for people to sit and chat, to read, watch the sun set, or enjoy the views? Adequate lighting? Do artwork and accent pieces highlight the decor? If the answers to these questions are no, it's time to redecorate.

On the other hand, your home may be a showplace, filled with fine antiques and delicate decor. Which can be good, or bad. As a B&B, your home must be user-friendly, sturdy, and comfortable. If you've got a spindly legged 18th century Windsor chair that's just for show, you can't tell your charming 250-pound guest he's not allowed to sit there. Your carpets will be tread on by countless feet and your designer comforters will bear more spills than you'd like to imagine.

Good Home Hunting

Perhaps the most exciting aspect of starting a B&B for many aspiring innkeepers is the hunt for that perfect historic home and its renovation. This can be a very expensive and time-consuming proposition, but if you've got the vision of an artist, the soul of a contractor, and the heart of an accountant, you'll be hard pressed to find any more gratifying way to go. Historic homes offer features not often found in today's modern structures—wood paneling, hardwood floors, crown moldings, plaster ornamentation, and fine detailing that cookie-cutter tract homes can't hope to match. When you renovate an old house, you touch the past and restore it to life. You create as well as re-create, and that's magical.

Cruising the Streets

Before you can work your magic, you need to hunt down that old house. Which means revisiting your market research and your own needs. What part of the country do you want to homestead? Do you need to stick within commuting distance of a spouse or partner's present job? Are you longing for schussable mountainsides or a beachcomber's paradise? Do you want to locate within a few hours' drive of the kids' colleges or your parents' homes?

Once you've homed in on an area that meets your needs and that your market research indicates will meet your income requirements, you can narrow down your search. Start by cruising the streets. Scope out a variety of neighborhoods—you may think you've already seen the sole "historic district" in town, but you'll often discover a bevy of other charming areas just slightly off the beaten path. They may be just two blocks over from Main Street, or tucked away at the quieter, less tourist-driven end of the beach, or hidden up in the hills above the town.

As you cruise, look for the following:

- *Signs of neighborhood prosperity.* Are homes and gardens well-maintained? Are shops and eateries open and bustling? Are parked cars of recent make and well-maintained?

- *Signs of neighborhood decay.* Are homes and yards neglected? Are shops and restaurants closed during prime business hours or out of business? Are parked cars elderly and run down?

Smart Tip

Look for homes that are unkempt and abandoned in nice, tidy neighborhoods. Then go to city hall, search out the owners, and contact them. They may be out-of-towners themselves who'll be delighted to have you purchase that noose around their necks for a lower-than-normal price.

- *Is there a surplus of for-sale or for-rent signs?* These can indicate a poor local economy.

- *Do passersby look cheerful and friendly?*

- *Unscientific but important: Do you like the neighborhood?* Does its architecture and ambience speak to you? If it doesn't speak to you, chances are it won't speak to the guests you're trying to attract.

Looky-Looing

Jot down the addresses of likely prospects sporting for-sale signs, as well as the real estate agencies' phone numbers. Then start calling. Ask for the home's price, number of bedrooms and bathrooms, age, square footage, and general condition. Some agents will be able to tell you all this off the tops of their heads; others won't even know which property you're talking about and will have to fumble for the bare basic of asking price. This is OK, because at this point you're just asking, being a sort of over-the-phone looky-loo.

The reason for this exercise is to give yourself a brief but comprehensive realtor-free overview of the area that may become your home. Real estate agents will often start off by showing you what they want to sell rather than what you want to buy. This method gives you a way to steer them in the right direction right off the bat. It also gives you a way to check whether neighborhood prices are way out of your range (or way in!) before you approach a realtor face-to-face.

Once you've identified a neighborhood or two—and even a house or two—that you're interested in, it's time to find a real estate broker. Pick up copies of the local home-buying freebies like *Homes & Land* as well as the Sunday edition of the local paper's real estate section. Look through them for ads heralding various agencies' top producers—the people who've sold a million or more dollars in properties within the past year. These are the people who are selling real estate for a living instead of as a hobby and are succeeding; they're the ones best capable of finding what you want and putting the deal together.

After you've identified a few top producers, call one and explain your needs—the neighborhood, type of house (or specific home), and the

Smart Tip
Tip...

If you're in an urban area, not all guests will arrive by car. Check into the availability of public transportation so guests aren't stranded once the taxi drops them at your door.

amount you're willing to spend. Make an appointment to meet in the agent's office and look at listings of potential properties that the agent will have printed out for you.

This is your chance to size up the agent as well as the properties. Has she listened to your requirements and chosen the types of houses you'll be interested in? Or is she pushing her own listings for which she'll get a larger commission but aren't what you want? Try to get a feel for her personality. Ask her to describe a few of her more challenging deals. Does she seem to be a creative negotiator who'll do whatever it takes to close a deal, down to taking a lower commission?

Make sure you enjoy each other's company. You'll spend a fair amount of time together looking at properties and going through some challenges of your own, including obtaining financing, appraisals, surveys, and city permits. You'll need an ally, not a mere drone with a key to local lockboxes.

If you feel the realtor won't work to negotiate a deal or you're just not simpatico, thank her for her time and go on to another on your list of top producers. Don't go out to look at properties with her anyway because, in real estate etiquette, you (or your business) belong to the agent who first shows you the home. Save that privilege for an agent with whom you really mesh.

Casing the Joint

Now that you've done all your preliminary legwork, found a neighborhood or two that you like and a real estate agent you can work with, it's time for the real fun—casing prospective properties. This is a task that's easier for some buyers than for others. Keep in mind that you're looking for a house to transform into a picture-perfect bed and breakfast. It's not likely to look like your ideal inn yet. (If you don't want to go through the fix-up process, skip ahead to page 64 and our exploration of purchasing an existing B&B.)

So you've got to exercise your imagination. Look at the home's bone structure and its potential. It doesn't matter if the walls are Pepto-Bismol pink or the bathroom fixtures look like refugees from a skid row flophouse. These are cosmetic elements that can be easily remedied. Doors that don't close properly, ominous-looking ceiling bulges that betray water leaks, cracked floor tiles, torn linoleum, sagging balconies, and décor that makes you cringe are all generally fixable without major structural repairs or astronomical price tags.

And, the upside to all these downers is that you can usually negotiate a much better price than if the house was in grade-A condition. As is, it scares away most potential buyers, which means that when you come along with a low-ball offer, they might be motivated to take it.

The Money Pit

Some houses, of course, are going to be true money pits, requiring more structural than cosmetic work, to the tune of thousands or even hundreds of thousands of dollars. This is why it's extremely important to have the property inspected by a professional. You can make an offer, but be sure it's contingent on a home inspection. This will cost you money, but it also means that if the inspection turns up anything you don't like, you can bow gracefully out of the contract without paying anything else. Home inspectors typically charge from $250 to $400, depending on the size of the home and going rates in the area.

A reputable home inspector will check out all the following items and more:

- Electrical wiring with frayed or cracked insulation; fuse boxes instead of circuit breakers
- Low water pressure throughout the house (guests won't appreciate a trickle instead of a shower)
- Lead plumbing
- Cracks or suspicious settling in foundations
- Floors that aren't level, lots of creaky floorboards or soft spots on floors
- Hardwood floors that have been sanded so often that the tongue-and-groove-boards are too thin to refinish
- Missing architectural detail that will be hard to match or replace, indoors or out
- Major cracks or gaps in tile shower pans
- Major termite or dry-rot damage
- Asbestos roofing, siding, or heating insulation
- Peeling lead-based paint

Where do you find a good home inspector? Check the local Yellow Pages or go directly to the American Society of Home Inspectors. You'll find contact information in the Appendix at the back of this book. As a rule of thumb, it's not a good idea to take a referral for a home inspector from your real estate agent; it's potentially a conflict of interest.

Checkin' It Out

Viewing a number of properties in succession can make your head spin, especially if you're only in town for a weekend and have to cram all that house-hunting into a short period before heading back to your present home and job. Your realtor will provide you with printed listings on each property, but they're only boilerplate forms with trifocal-demanding print and not a lot of detail. Instead of relying strictly on your memory, use the "House-Hunting Checklist" below to note both your requirements and the details of each property. Make copies for each house, and take them along on a clipboard for handy note-taking. It also helps to bring along a camera or video camera.

This checklist will also help you weed out impossible properties before you go to the expense of hiring a home inspector. If a house has lead plumbing or knob-and-tube wiring, for instance, you may want to pass on it as these are both danger signs that are very expensive to change. If your budget is small, you may not want to get involved with such a house.

You may not be able to spot some of the items on this list, like whether the house is on city sewer or a septic tank. You'll have to ask the owner or real estate agent. Some items, like the knob-and-tube wiring, may require you to stick your head into the attic to check. You should be able to tell the difference between this and conduit, and between copper pipe and plastic PVC. If you can't and the owner doesn't know, ask him to find out.

House-Hunting Checklist

1. House address: _____

_____

2. Listing price: _____

3. Architectural style: _____

4. Age of home: _____

5. On National Register of Historic Homes? _____

_____

6. Is there an architectural review board? _____

7. General overall condition: _____

8. What is the age and condition of the roof? _____

_____

House-Hunting Checklist, continued

9. Do you see cracks or sags in the foundation or the side of the building?

    _____

10. Do porches or columns show signs of fatigue? _____

11. Electrical: Does the main panel have:

    *   Circuit breakers _____

    *   Fuses _____ *(Fuses will have to be changed out and the electrical
        service more than likely upgraded considerably.)*

    Is the wiring:

    *   Knob-and-tube _____

    *   Romex wire _____

    *   Conduit (in a metal pipe) _____

        *(Conduit and Romex are preferable; knob-and-tube is old and will prob-
        ably have to be changed at great expense.)*

    *   Is there at least one outlet per wall in each room? _____

12. Plumbing:

    Is the house on city sewer or septic? _____

    *(A septic tank's drain field may mean there's less room for expansion, plus
    there's more maintenance and the likelihood of plumbing trouble.)*

    *   If septic, can you have it tied into the city sewer? _____

    *   If not, what is the condition of the drain field? _____

    *   How many guests and family will it handle? _____

    Is the house on city water, or does it have a well? _____

    *   If well water, can you be tied into city water? _____

    *   What is the condition of the well? _____

    *   How many guests and family will it handle? _____

    What kind of pipes does the house have?

    *   Copper _____

    *   PVC _____

    *   Galvanized steel _____

    *   Lead _____ *(If lead, you'll have to change out the entire system
        at great expense.)*

House-Hunting Checklist, continued

13. Curb appeal: _____

14. Square footage: _____

15. Number of bedrooms: _____

16. Number of baths: _____

17. Additional bath or bedroom capability: _____

18. Separate owners' quarters: _____

19. If not, is owners' suite separated from guest rooms? _____

20. Den or other room that can be turned into private family living area? __

   _____

21. Any fireplaces? _____

22. Parking situation: _____

23. Is there room to add parking if necessary? _____

24. Size of garage, if any: _____

25. Land for expansion in future? _____

   _____

26. Is the kitchen spacious enough to prepare food for guests and family?

   _____

27. If you'll have six or more guest rooms, you'll need at least one that's wheelchair-accessible. Will this be a problem? _____

   _____

28. Flood zone? _____

29. What do I really like about the house? _____

   _____

30. What do I really dislike about it? _____

   _____

Negotiating the Deal

Sooner or later you'll find that must have property, the one you fall in love with. Terrific. But it doesn't mean your work is done. You and your realtor will now have to formulate an offer. If it's a seller's market (with more eager buyers than there are homes for sale), you may find yourself paying full price and being happy you got the house. If it's a buyer's market where real estate sales are sluggish, you've got negotiating possibilities.

Either way, you'll want to consider—and spell out—all the following elements when writing up the sales contract.

- *Financing*. You'll want the contract to be subject to your ability to obtain an acceptable loan within a given time period. If you can't get terms you can live with from the bank, you can bow out of the contract. Keep in mind that banks tend to get even pickier than usual when lending on commercial properties. They'll require a 25 percent down payment compared to the customary 20 percent or less for residential loans. They'll insist on 15- to 20-year amortized notes that will have to be (hopefully) renewed—with a corresponding slew of new paperwork—every three to five years. In comparison, conventional home loans are typically written with 15- or 30-year notes, lower interest rates, and no renewal clauses. You may be able to get a residential loan if you'll run a homestay or smaller B&B where the bank will view the property as your residence with some supplemental income. If you have concerns about which category you'll fall into, consult your attorney before approaching the bank.

- *Appraisal*. You'll want (and the bank will demand) an appraisal of the property by a qualified real estate appraiser. This can be good, as when the house appraises for more than the sales price, and you know you got a terrific deal. Or it can be bad. If your intended purchase is a potential gem but also a major fixer that only you and the seller can yet see the beauty in, and it appraises for less than the sales price, that unimaginative bank will only lend 80 percent of the appraised price or 80 percent of the sales price, whichever is lower.

- *Inspections*. As we've already explored, you'll want to have a qualified home inspector go over the plumbing, heating and cooling, electrical systems, foundation, roof, and other structural elements. You'll also want a termite inspection; these can usually be done by any local pest control company.

- *Zoning and licensing*. Your contract should also be contingent on your ability to obtain a zoning permit or variance and any pertinent city or county licenses—if you can't get these, you can't have a B&B.

- *Building permit*. If you'll need to do a lot of remodeling to transform the house into a B&B, you'll want to know that you can get a building permit.

- *Assignment*. Stipulate that the sales contract is assignable to another entity. Then, if you choose to transfer the contract to the partnership or corporation you'll form (more on this in Chapter 5), you can do so.
- *Sale of your home*. You may want to make the successful purchase of the new property contingent on the sale of your present digs. This way, if your present home doesn't sell, you're not stuck with two mortgages and you may be able to use the proceeds from the one as a down payment on the other.

Smart Tip

Tip...

How much commission will you pay when you sell your present home? Real estate agents typically get 5 to 7 percent of the sales price. But that figure can usually be negotiated—many agents (and brokers) would rather take a lower commission to get the property sold than lose the deal.

Renovations

OK, you've decided your present home is terrific B&B material—except it needs a couple of extra bathrooms. Or you've bought a house that will make the perfect bed and breakfast—once you bump out the kitchen, add new appliances, and convert the screened-in sleeping porch into an owners' suite. Or you found a historic mansion with excellent bone structure and oodles of character—except that the roof leaks, those great old columns holding up the portico are sagging, and there's more lathe than plaster on the lathe-and-plaster walls. It's time to talk remodeling and renovations.

Bright Idea

David and Marilyn Lewis in Fort Worth, Texas, have been able to renovate their historic home and accommodate guests while construction is underway. They first had work done on two guest cottages at the back of the property and then used the cottages to generate room revenues while they worked on the house.

If you're up-close and personal with all those fix-up shows on *Home & Garden Television*, you'll be in heaven. Here's your chance to shine. But you've got a lot of decisions to make before you forge ahead.

First off, decide just how much remodeling work needs to be done, how much needs to be done immediately, and which items can be shelved for a later time. (Use the checklist on page 118 in Chapter 7.) Renovations are time-consuming, wearying, and, of course, expensive. "Construction will cost twice as much and take a lot longer than planned," advise Bill and Sandra Wayne in Missouri, who have first-hand experience. They renovated their 1867 farmhouse by adding a modern addition for their private quarters and making space for HVAC (heating, ventilation, and air conditioning) systems and indoor plumbing.

"Bump up any expenses by 25 percent," adds Nancy Sandstrom in Wisconsin, who with husband Steve added two guest rooms to their original four-room property and are now at the start of another remodel, which will take them down to five guest rooms but add an additional common room.

You'll want to put must-haves like indoor plumbing and private baths ahead of wish-list noncritical items like a greenhouse window for the kitchen or a balcony off your personal quarters.

Keep in mind that, while you may be able to overlook drywall dust on every flat surface and workers' radios blasting country favorites over the house at 7 in the morning, your guests won't have the same indifference. So you'll have to get the major renovations finished before you open or during your off-season when you'll be able to juggle work schedules around less frequent guest stays.

Generals and Contractors

Before you break out the power tools and muscle liniment and start your own remodeling job, you'll need to consider whether those renovations are legal. If you make any sort of structural changes, you'll need a city or county building permit. In some locales, you can't make any exterior changes without the permission of the architectural review board. (For more information, see page 76 in Chapter 5.) And some local governments will only allow you to do the work yourself if the building is your own residence. If it's a commercial structure, you must hire a licensed contractor.

DIY Delight

If you're a weekend warrior who's handy with a hammer and loves tackling construction projects, you may want to tackle the remodel yourself. Going the DIY (do-it-yourself) route is far less expensive than hiring a contractor, but unless you can enlist an army of assistants, it will also take longer. And since you'll need to get up and running before you start earning revenues, time is money.

DIY, however, can be extremely rewarding. It can also be fun! Enlist friends and family for renovation parties. Let them help paint, wallpaper, or plant the garden; then top off the weekend with a hot and hearty stew that's been simmering on the stove all afternoon or a burger bash on the back patio grill.

Deciding to turn the job over to a contractor opens up yet more avenues for investigation. You don't want to be one of those horror stories everyone's heard about contractors who are more "con" than professional builder. Whether you'll hire a general contractor responsible for every phase of your remodel who will hire subcontractors to do tile, drywall or plaster, plumbing or roofing; act as your own general and hire subs; or contract out a single specialty like plumbing the bathroom and do the rest of the work yourself, you'll need to do your homework.

> **Beware!**
> Make sure all subcontractors and suppliers have been paid by the general contractor before you sign off on a job. Unpaid subs and suppliers can file a mechanic's lien on your property, which means you can't sell the property until they get paid, usually by you—even if you don't find out they were stiffed until years later.

Start your search for reliable, reputable contractors by asking residential and business neighbors who've had remodeling done for recommendations. Check with local home improvement centers, your real estate agent and bank loan officer, as well as local architects and designers. Your town architectural review board or historical preservation society can probably provide you with some excellent choices. If you need to start off with an architect, you can use the same sources.

Ask for a list of references and then check them out. Before you sign a contract, make sure you've covered labor and material costs and the length of time the job is expected to take. Find out how many other projects the contractor is handling at the same time and what their scope is—you don't want your job to take a back seat because the contractor is more interested in remodeling Madonna's kitchen or is already overwhelmed with too many jobs already in progress.

Buying an Existing B&B

If your present home doesn't fit your B&B parameters or you want to move to a new location and you're not a buyer/fixer-upper personality who loves the scents of paint and sawdust, you've got another option. And that's to purchase a bed and breakfast that's already in operation.

If the B&B you choose is currently up and running and is doing so successfully, this option actually has several things going for it. It will come complete with advertising in place and a fair amount of repeat business. The present owners will have worked the bugs out and can pass their secrets along to you. And unless they're operating under a special, nontransferable zoning variance or business license, you don't have to worry about being turned down.

As added bonuses, banks—always ultra-conservative—are much more likely to write a loan on a business that shows a positive cash flow right now than on a private residence-turned-B&B that they'll be inclined to view as your uneducated and unprofitable dabble. And if the bank still won't lend the amount you need, a motivated owner may carry back a note, letting you pay off a second deed or mortgage to him to seal the deal.

The downside, of course, is that you'll pay more than you would if you bought a private home. You're buying not only the physical structure but the fixtures, quite possibly the furnishings, the office equipment, supplies and amenities, and the goodwill, or benefits of a good reputation and smart marketing.

Surfing for Sales

How do you find bed and breakfasts for sale? That's easy. You'll find scads of tantalizing listings in B&B magazines and online resources including inn consultants and inn sales web sites like InnkeepingForSale.com. Check out the "Inn Sales" section in the Appendix at the back of this book. Surfing listings is fun—and addictive—as you discover tempting properties all over the country and even in foreign climes.

Prices are as varied as the properties themselves. You'll find charming homestays or small B&Bs for under $300,000, elegant mansions with eight or more rooms for $1 million-plus (or more), and everything in between. Asking prices vary not only with the type and size of the property but also with their locations.

Just as in the residential market, the asking price of a B&B is just that, the price the owner is asking—not necessarily what it's actually worth. Some people have greatly inflated ideas of their property's value. To get a true picture, you'll have to use your real estate broker or inn consultant's informed opinion, your market research statistics, and your own intuition.

Keep in mind that a B&B that's less than three years old isn't likely to have much of a business reputation or following. And it may not have a lot of advertising under its belt either. B&B guests often rely on hard copy guidebooks as well as online web sites to lead them to the best inns, and most guidebooks are only printed once a year. Unless it's a large property, you may want to consider a newbie inn in the same category as a private home.

Private Investigations

That existing B&B may be as charming as it appears, but then again, it may not be. And you

Smart Tip

Go online with the National Association of the Remodeling Industry (www.nari.org), which provides tips on starting and working through your remodeling project as well as finding and interviewing a professional remodeling contractor.

don't want to take over someone else's money pit. So you'll need to be even nosier when purchasing an existing B&B than when buying a home.

Ask why the present owners are selling. Then do a little private investigation—which means diplomatically asking neighbors, neighboring business owners, and the inn's service people or suppliers about the economic climate and the B&B's reputation in the area. If the bed and breakfast uses a reservation service, try to find out—again diplomatically—what its rep is there. Is it one of their bestsellers or a problem child?

Smart Tip

Inn and B&B sales web sites often feature "Wanted" listings. Here you can post an ad for the B&B of your dreams, including size, price, and location, to attract innkeepers who just may decide to sell—to you.

You'll want your contract to give you the same outs as a contract for a private home, as we explored earlier in this chapter. You should also include a clause in the contract giving you time to peruse and approve the following items—another out if you don't like what you see. Besides the usual market research criteria, you'll want to carefully examine:

- Guest registers for the past three years and the year-to-date. These will give you an accurate picture of occupancy and room rates as well as how the B&B fares from season to season.
- Schedule or calendar showing all upcoming reservations with deposits
- Advertising, marketing, and promotional methods and campaigns, including current and past brochures, print ads, press releases, or articles in magazines or other publications
- A list of advertising, marketing, and promotional venues, including any reservation services in use, along with contact names and phone numbers
- A list of suppliers and service people along with contact names and phone numbers
- Names of managerial or supervisory employees, if any, their pay rates and duties
- Payroll statements for the past three years and the year-to-date so you can evaluate the turnover rate of staff or seasonal employees
- Income-and-expense statements, sales tax records, and other financial records for the past three years and the year-to-date
- Tax returns for the past three years
- Business licenses, resale license, liquor license (if applicable), permits, inspection schedules, reports, contracts, and all other records and paperwork. Check to make sure licenses, permits, contracts, and inspections are up-to-date.

- A list of all inventory, tools, equipment, fixtures, and furnishings as well as the seller's statement of their worth. Verify current worth for yourself; used kitchen equipment, for instance, loses its value quickly. A state-of-the-art Belgian waffle iron that cost $250 new can plummet to $40 once it's a year old. Be sure to check that all equipment is in good working order. Ask to see warranties on any equipment new enough to be under warranty.

- A list of receivables—monies due the business from reservation services or other sources—and a list of payables—monies the business owes to suppliers or other sources. These revenues and expenses will have to be divided up after the sale according to whether they were due or payable before or after you take over.

And this isn't all! You'll also want to consider the present state of the B&B from the perspective of your plans for it. If you envision major remodeling or redecorating, how will these expenses affect your bottom line? Will it be cheaper in the long run to start from scratch?

Cast a critical eye on the furnishings; check for wear and tear on towels, linens, bedspreads or comforters, drapes, rugs, and upholstered as well as wood furniture. Are they new and snappy or looking a bit threadbare? Find out when they were purchased. Carpets in lodging establishments have a normal life of four to five years, seven if you're lucky. Chairs and sofas can be expected to survive about five years—those with pull-out beds not as long. Quality hard goods—desks, dressers, armoires, and the like—should last 10 to 15 years.

A New Lease Inn Life

OK, your present home just won't do as a B&B and however much you drool over those for-sale listings of private residences and existing inns, you can't afford to purchase. Not to worry. There's yet another option available—leasing a bed and breakfast. You can structure the deal as a straight lease or as a lease with an option to purchase at a later date.

As with any other real estate transaction, you'll want to have your real estate agent, inn consultant, or attorney look over and approve the lease before you sign on the dotted line. While you're hammering out the details with the owner, be sure you deal with these elements:

Smart Tip

Sit in on operations for a few days. This will give you a good chance to monitor the volume of business and the clientele, and to pick up valuable pointers on innkeeping.

- *Duration.* How long will you want to lease the inn? Typical time frames are three-, five-, 10- and 20-year periods. A long lease can protect your interests, which is grand if you find you love where you are and what you're doing, but disastrous if you decide you detest it. Be sure to structure periodic renewal or termination clauses so you can exit gracefully if you so choose.

- *Purchase option.* If you want to buy the B&B, here's your chance. Spell out the agreed-upon sales price and the time period in which you plan to purchase. You may structure the lease so that a portion of your monthly payments go toward the down payment. Or you may build in a clause giving you first right of refusal if the owner decides to sell the property.

- *Sales percentages.* Commercial leases typically require the lessee (that's you) to pay a percentage of his monthly revenues to the lessor in addition to the monthly rent. Since the lodging business is seasonal and takes time to build, this is probably not in your best interest unless the B&B is already operating with a high year-round occupancy rate or the monthly rent is very low.

- *Repairs and maintenance.* Make sure you spell out in the contract whether you or the owner pays for repairs and maintenance—anything from slow drains and burst pipes to faulty kitchen equipment and monthly pest control.

- *Renovations and upgrades.* Build in a clause for renovations and upgrades. If you and the owner work as a team to improve the B&B with higher-room-rate items like private baths, whirlpool tubs, or fireplaces, you'll need to specify who pays for the improvements.

- *Property sale.* Your lease should stipulate that, in the event of a sale where you're not the purchaser, the new owner must honor your lease. If you don't have a lease option, be sure to add in a right of first refusal.

The Roof Over Your Beds
Legal and Business Structures

For a successful B&B, you need a sound and sturdy structure with a roof that doesn't leak and a foundation that doesn't sag. You also need an equally sound and sturdy legal and business structure. In this chapter, we'll explore everything necessary to achieve that, from designing a business name and image to developing a business entity to dealing with local governments as well as with Uncle Sam.

In with the Inn Crowd

Christening your bed and breakfast is an extremely gratifying part of your start-up. Once you do so, you feel that you've got a real business instead of just a private home. You're an innkeeper! And ready to be in with the inn crowd.

If you purchase an existing B&B with a terrific reputation, you won't need to think up a name—you'll already have one. And changing it will only confuse repeat guests and sabotage all that advertising and marketing that's already in place—which was part of what you paid for!

If you're starting from scratch, however, you'll want to carefully consider your name. It's the first thing most guests will ever see or hear—your identity on a web page packed with names of inns or the words from a reservation service agent's lips. You want your B&B's name to paint an instantaneous picture for prospective guests—elegant or playful, secluded or citified, historic or contemporary, or something else completely unique that will captivate them.

So where do you start? Try these brainstorming ideas:

- Name your bed and breakfast for a scenic or meteorological feature of your area, like Shorecliff Cottage, Painted Rock Bed & Breakfast, or Windy City Inn.
- Aim for a historic connection to your area, like High Cotton B&B or Gold Panner's Bed & Breakfast. Some innkeepers incorporate the age of their home directly into its name, like 1879 Haven House.
- Use the name of your historic home's former owner, like the General Lee House or the Amos Wingate Mansion. Don't use your own name; Brenda's B&B and Joe Jones' Inn don't make a statement.
- Choose a feature of your house or grounds, like Seven Gables B&B, Honeysuckle Cottage, or Tranquility Inn.
- Use the worksheet on page 71 to help you decide on a name for your B&B.

Name of the Game

Once you've decided on a name for your bed and breakfast, you'll need to register it. This helps ensure that no one else in your area is already using your name and that no one else in your area can legally take your business name at a later date. It also gives your B&B its first legal status. This is an important step—banks won't give you a business account without a fictitious business name statement, also called

Brainstorming Your B&B Name

List three ideas based on your area's scenic features.

1. _____

2. _____

3. _____

List three ideas based on your home's history or property features

1. _____

2. _____

3. _____

After you've decided which name you like best, have you:

❑ Tried it aloud to make sure it's easily understood and pronounced? (Has it passed muster with your family? Have you had a friend call to see how it sounds over the phone?)

❑ Checked your local Yellow Pages to make sure the same or similar name is not already listed?

❑ Checked with your local business name authority to make sure it's available?

a dba, for "doing business as." And without a business account, many suppliers won't deal with you.

Getting your dba is easy, although the process varies a bit in different regions of the country. Some states have embraced technology allowing you to do this search online. Others still allow you to do it the old-fashioned way if you prefer. In the state of Florida, for instance, you can call the office of the Secretary of State and, after a lengthy period on hold, are given the opportunity to check on up to three potential business names. If there's already a Pirate's Cove B&B, or whichever was your first pick, you go on to your next choice and then your next. When you find one that hasn't already been appropriated, the Secretary's office sends you a registration form. You mail back the completed form, the registration fee, and a form from your local newspaper verifying that you've advertised your dba for one week. In return, you receive your business name certificate—your B&B is official!

In other areas of the country, you might simply pop down to your city or county clerk's office, thumb through the roster of business names, and then complete the registration procedure at the clerk's window. To find out the procedure in your area, call your county clerk's office. The classified department of your local newspaper and your bank's commercial officer should also be able to steer you in the right direction. Filing fees for dbas typically range from $10 to $100—in some areas, the newspaper will take care of all the paperwork for you for an additional small fee.

Giving You the Business

Besides your fictitious business license, you'll also need to apply for a number of other city or county licenses and permits. Some are required for any business, others are geared toward the hospitality industry. Don't ignore any of them. Even if you're a homestay with two or three guest rooms, you're still a business, and local, state, and federal authorities will view you as such—with unpleasant consequences from fines to shutting you down if you're caught running your operation illegally.

First up is the business license. This is just what it sounds like, permission to do business within the city limits, but it's just as much a way for the local governing body to know who and where you are so it can attach taxes. The license fee is nominal and so is the paperwork. Where things can get sticky is that, once you've applied for the business license, the city checks how you fit into its zoning and parking ordinances.

Zone Out or Zone Inn

Which brings us to the all-important issue of zoning. Zoning ordinances vary tremendously from one locale to another and are typically regulated by the city or county planning commission or planning board. Some municipalities, operating under the quirky assumption that boarding houses and tourist homes are still common, will consider a homestay or smaller B&B a residential business and let it go at that. Others feel that any bed and breakfast is a commercial enterprise that belongs in a business district. Still others, unfamiliar with the B&B concept, decide on a case-by-case basis.

Some municipalities include other issues besides location in their zoning ordinances. Some limit the number of days guests can stay per visit—typically seven or 14 days—as a means of ensuring that they remain short-term guests instead of long-term tenants. Some cities limit the number of guest rooms allowed in a residential neighborhood. Some prohibit cooking facilities in guest rooms, which means no kitchenettes allowed.

If your B&B is located in a business district, you'll probably pass with flying colors. But if your neighborhood isn't zoned for a bed and breakfast, you'll have to apply for a variance or a conditional use permit.

This generally means that you appear before the planning commission as a star in your very own courtroom drama. You explain how your business will operate and why it won't change or harm the tenor of the neighborhood. If your town is B&B-oriented, with a number of bed and breakfasts already in operation, you shouldn't meet with much opposition. But if you'll be a pioneer in the local field, you may also need to explain (as we explored in Chapter 2) how bed and breakfasts actually improve neighborhoods.

Parking Signs

Riding shotgun with the question of zoning are the parking and signage issues. Most cities stipulate that businesses allow adequate off-street parking for a set number of cars, typically one space for each guest room. They'll also want extra spaces for your own family vehicles. Depending on your specific location, you may be able to get around this by suggesting that guests can park in nearby public lots or in business parking lots or on the street after hours.

As for signage, you may not be allowed to post any sign at all if you're in a residential area. Which is fine if you'll go the homestay route and/or you don't want any walk-in traffic. But if you're planning on an inn-sized operation that will attract passersby, you'll have a hard time making your presence known.

Mimosas in the Morning

You may choose to serve guests sherries in the parlor as an evening ritual or champagne-and-orange juice mimosas with a holiday breakfast. In some states, this is fine; in others, you'll need a liquor license.

Beer-and-wine licenses are typically easy to apply for and to obtain, but licenses to serve hard liquor are extremely expensive and difficult to get. In some areas, the only way is to buy a license from an existing business that's closing its doors.

So before you do the champagne cocktail or wine-and-cheese thing, check with your state alcoholic beverage control board, otherwise known as the ABC. To locate yours, do an online search or look in the white pages of your phone directory under state agencies.

Even in business districts, some municipalities can get sticky about signage. They may insist that your sign be placed a set distance back from the curb or be placed only directly on your building. For most B&Bs, which prefer discreet, low-key signage anyway, this is not a problem. But it is a matter you should check into before you have a sign made.

B & Be Healthy

While you're tackling the planning commission or board, you'll also want to check into your local health department's food safety regulations. These can vary considerably from state to state and from region to region; in fact, they may not even be called a health department or board of health. In Florida, for instance, the regulatory agency is called the Department of Business and Professional Regulations.

In Wisconsin, innkeeper Nancy Sandstrom reports, bed and breakfast hosts with up to eight guest rooms must hold a state license and live on-site. A commercial kitchen isn't required although there are food safety regulations to adhere to.

In some areas, B&Bs avoid food safety monitoring because breakfasts are considered part of the room rate instead of meals that guests pay independently for. If you live in one of these areas, you'll still have to apply for a permit if you charge a supplemental fee for things like picnic lunches or candlelit suppers.

Bill and Sandra Wayne in Missouri provide home-cooked country breakfasts but no other meals. "We did other meals when we started, but not any more since it's too much work for the revenue and it requires excessive government intrusion," the couple explains. "We do provide an evening snack."

Some areas require you to serve—even for breakfast—only foods that come pre-wrapped and unhandled by you, like packaged sweet rolls, individual boxes or bags of cereals, and individual portions of butter, jams, and creamer. This will put a definite damper on your gourmet breakfasts.

Here your only other option is to install commercial kitchen facilities that meet all food safety requirements. This can be an extremely expensive proposition, involving three-bowl sinks, commercial dishwashers, and drain and dry areas, specialized ranges and hoods, and even special storage units for your pantry.

Fees for food safety permits typically start at $25 and go up depending on what type of operation and equipment you have. They may also require you to apply for and then take classes to obtain a food handler's permit.

General Safety

The health department (or whatever it's called in your state) will also do an initial inspection, followed by routine checks, to make sure you've got general as well as food safety under control. They'll check to see that you have smoke detectors, fire extinguishers, or other required fire safety equipment installed, that you have adequate outdoor night lighting, that bathrooms are clean, and that walkways and stairways are sturdy and unobstructed.

If you have a swimming pool or hot tub, they'll check the water quality and chemical levels, make sure you've got safety features like ladders, steps, and underwater lights, and even specify the size and placement of those tiles that tell the water's depth.

Building Department

If you'll do that remodeling or build a new B&B, then you'll get to know your local building department—especially if you do any portion of the work yourself. First, of course, you'll get those plans approved and get a building permit.

Once the permit is issued, you can start work. But you (or your contractor) will have to notify your assigned building inspector at various stages of progress. The inspector will come out, verify that the wiring or plumbing or whatever is up to code and give you an A—or, in other words, sign off that stage of the job and allow you to go on to the next, until the entire project is completed and signed off.

In cases of major rehabilitation or new construction, you can't legally move into the property until the project is signed off and the building department issues a certificate

The All-Clear

In some areas, you'll need an all-clear from the local fire department as well as the health department. Regulations vary from one city or county to another and can also vary depending on whether you'll have new construction, will remodel or will use your existing home.

No matter who or where you are, you'll need (and want) smoke detectors in strategic locations. These can be battery-operated, which means you'll have to monitor battery freshness on a routine basis, or hard-wired, which involves electrical installation and is the preferred choice of safety professionals. You'll also need (and want) commercial-grade fire extinguishers in the kitchen and at least one on each floor.

Your local fire department may also require safety features like ceiling-mounted sprinklers, one-hour fire doors and at least two easily accessible exits. In many cases, they'll only require these in new or renovated structures but not in existing structures.

of occupancy. This is a red-letter day—the power company comes out and hooks up your electricity, throws the switch, and you've got a B&B!

Architectural Review

Some areas have architectural review boards that stringently monitor and critique any proposed changes to building exteriors as well as any new buildings. For some towns, like Beaufort, South Carolina, and Savannah, Georgia, this is a way to ensure that their rich historical heritage isn't sullied by somebody who decides a contemporary glass box or Swiss chalet would look good in between antebellum mansions, or that he'll add a Miami South Beach-style addition onto a pre-Civil War cottage.

But you'll also find architectural review boards in newer communities that are concerned about keeping up appearances as well as in private subdivisions and homeowners' associations. They may limit your B&B to a particular architectural style like Spanish, Caribbean, or local turn-of-the-20th-century. And they may even rule on what color you can paint your front door or window shutters.

Americans with Disabilities Act

While you're planning your renovations and upgrades, you'll need to consider the federal Americans with Disabilities Act, more conveniently known as ADA. This act concerns itself (and you) with making public buildings accessible and enjoyable by people who are visually impaired, hearing-impaired, and wheelchair-bound or otherwise physically challenged. In typical government fashion, the ruling is so complex that the regulating body, the Department of Justice, limits its ADA home page on the web to a suggestion: Call a given toll-free number and ask for specific advice for your situation.

The basics for a B&B, however, are fairly simple. If you have five guest rooms or fewer and you live on the property, you're exempt from the law. If you have six or more guest rooms, you'll need to make just one room out of each 25 rooms disability-friendly. And if you have no more than 14 employees, you don't need to concern yourself with ADA employment requirements.

The law can get fuzzy, depending on whether you're building new construction, substantially remodeling, or have an existing historic home. It doesn't necessarily insist that you install elevators or permanent wheelchair

> **Beware!**
> Architectural review boards may restrict not only the look of your home but also its size and dimensions. Some specify only single-family dwellings—this means you'll have to ask for a variance. Some limit the number of stories you can add, especially where you may block somebody else's view.

ramps all over the house. But it does expect you to devise some, at least temporary, disability-friendly measures. For specifics as they apply to you, contact your local building department. To get an idea of what may be required, take a look at the following:

Physically Challenged

- The first—and possibly simplest—thing you'll need is a portable or permanent ramp that gives guests access to your B&B.
- You'll need a special parking space that's 14 feet wide by 18 feet deep and close to your entrance rather than at the far end of the back lot.
- Doorways to common rooms should be at least 32 inches wide with low thresholds so wheelchairs don't encounter unintentional bumpers. This also includes doorways in ADA guest rooms and bathrooms. Door handles may need to be lower than normal and lever-style instead of knobs.
- Guest bedrooms need tabletops and desktops 27 inches to 29 inches off the floor with 19 inches of knee space to allow room for wheelchairs. Beds need to be wheelchair-accessible height and not so close to the wall or other furniture that there's no room for the wheelchair to drive right up. Closet bars, clothes hooks, and thermostats should be low enough to reach from a wheelchair.
- Bathrooms need raised toilet seats, portable bath seats, grab bars, lever-style faucets, higher sinks, and a full-length mirror you can see yourself in from a wheelchair. Don't forget turnaround space in guest rooms and bathrooms—wheelchairs need room to maneuver.

Visually Impaired

- Exterior walkways should be well-lit (which is a good idea for your nonimpaired guests as well).
- Printed information from guest rules to menus should be available in large-print and Braille formats.
- You'll need contrast-color strips along top and bottom steps of stairways.
- They'll need a verbal description of room layout and surroundings, especially unusually low doorways or uneven walkways.

Hearing Impaired

- You'll need a TDD, or telecommunications display device, for making reservations and giving guests telephone access.

- You'll need to have closed-captioning on your televisions. (Most new sets come equipped with closed-captioning options.)
- Your guests will need to be attuned to smoke detectors, knocks on doors, alarm clocks, and ringing telephones. You can provide separate signalers, like flashing lights and bed shakers for each, or you can purchase one portable gadget that alerts hearing-impaired guests to all these things.

Taxing Issues

Now that you've made yourself accountable to what probably seems like every governing body known to innkeeping, you may think you're done with the red-tape thing. Almost—but not quite. There's still the irksome matter of taxes.

Paying Staff

If you'll hire employees, you'll need to apply to Uncle Sam for an employee identification number or EIN so you can send in your payroll taxes. If you'll operate as a partnership or corporation, the IRS will provide you with an EIN by phone or fax—all

Bedtime Tax

Most states, cities, and counties levy sales taxes on products or services sold for profit. These can include anything you might sell to guests from your own B&B recipe books, to guidebooks written by others, to your own B&B-labeled luxury bathrobes, to gift items or toiletries you offer from your shop or front desk. Some areas may tax the meal portion of your room rate. Many locales—especially those in tourist-heavy areas—also collect a bed tax, a special tax on room rates.

It's important to note that all these taxes aren't revenues—even though guests pay them to you, you're only a collection facility. You turn them over to the proper authorities on a quarterly, or sometimes monthly, basis. And once you start reporting sales and bed taxes, you don't stop. Even in a month or quarter when you have no sales, you still turn in the paperwork.

Sales and bed taxes are yet another murky area in which what gets taxed, at what rate, and who gets to collect (city, county, state, or all three) vary with your particular locale, so consult your accountant for details.

you have to do is call the toll-free number you can find in your white pages or online under IRS. If you'll operate as a sole proprietorship (see more on this in "Laying the Foundation" on page 81 in this chapter), you can use your Social Security number.

You'll also need to be accountable to the state for unemployment insurance taxes, for which you'll need a state employer identification number. For more information, call the local branch of your state employment development office, or check with your accountant.

Even if you do all the work yourself and don't hire a single soul, you'll still have to turn "payroll tax" money over to the IRS on a quarterly basis. This is called self-employment tax; it goes into your Social Security kitty, and there's no getting around it. For more information, call the IRS or, better yet, talk to your accountant.

Out of the Woods

OK, you're out of the woods with all the government stuff! Time to get back to more entertaining aspects of running your B&B. You've chosen a name, but you'll also want a domain name, the www.whatever link that prospective guests can key in or click on to access your web site.

And you definitely want a web site. "Internet!" is what Bill and Sandra Wayne in Warrensburg, Missouri, say when asked what's their most successful advertising medium. "Our own domain plus a selection of other guides accounts for about 82 percent of our business."

Registering for a domain name is easy but can require a bit of ingenuity. Like a dba, no two companies can have the same domain name, so you'll have to think up several versions of the name you want in case one's already been taken.

Here's what you do: Go into your web browser and type in www.networksolutions.com. Now you're at the (surprise!) Network Solutions web site, which is very user friendly—and fun! Following the easy directions, check to see if the domain name you've chosen has been taken. If it has, choose another or devise a variation. If, for instance, there's already a www.gullcottage.com, try gullcottagesi (for Sullivan's Island) or gullcottageonline—whatever works and makes sense.

When you find a permutation that's available, register online. The cost—if you already have a web host on which to put up your site—is $35 for a one-year registration, or $40 for a

Stat Fact

Think tax time isn't fun? Think again. One out of five adult Americans said they plan to use all or part of their income tax refund to fund their vacations in a recent survey by the Travel Industry Association of America.

one-year reservation (if you want to reserve a name, but you don't plan to use it right away). For more on doing business on the internet, see Chapter 11.

Bed and Breakfast Imagery

You've carefully chosen the name of your B&B to instill a particular image in guests' minds and inspire a desire to visit. But there's more to image than a name. Your visual image—the colors, graphics, typefaces, and paper stocks you choose for everything from stationery to brochures to mailing labels—will play a leading role in your guests' perception of your inn.

Study other B&Bs' printed materials and web sites to see how they've developed an image and a style; then design your own. If your inn will target romantics, for instance, you might choose a pink-and-gold theme embellished with hearts and cupids. If you're on the sea, you might go breezily nautical with ropelike borders and anchor accents. Or you could cater to families with kids (and the kid in every guest) with a playful design of sand pails and sand castles. If your home's history is its essence, you might feature a line drawing "portrait," along with a suggestion of cobblestone walks or horse-drawn carriages.

Despite your web site, you'll send brochures, reservation confirmation letters, and other materials to guests by mail. You can design and print everything from letterhead and business cards to envelopes with your own computer system, so it doesn't have to be expensive—but it does need to carry out your theme. Use papers with weight, class, and distinction:

- Letterhead paper weight should be about 24 pounds—not the copier-grade see-through stuff that's 20 pounds. You might try a style that's specially textured for added interest.

- Business cards that you print from your computer come in sheets with each card perforated for easy tear-out. Go for stock with fine perforations so they look professionally printed, not the stuff with raggedy "punched" edges.

- Envelopes should match your letterhead and your business cards.

If you'll do bulk mailings for market research purposes, as part of a direct-mail blitz (see more on this in Chapter 11), or plaster local visitors centers with brochures, you may want to go with a professional printer instead of printing each piece yourself.

> ## Smart Tip
> Print shop prices can vary from store to store and even from day to day, depending on paper prices, what the printer has in stock, and how many other jobs he's got on tap. Quick-copy centers like Kinko's and Office Depot's in-house operations can often offer better prices than local vendors—but not always. Do your homework!

Laying the Foundation

A primary element in the foundation of your B&B is its legal structure. To keep that taxing arm of Uncle Sam content, you must choose to operate as either a sole proprietorship, a partnership, or a corporation. While many innkeepers go with the simplest and least expensive version, the sole proprietorship, this is not always the best option for everybody.

You may choose, for example, to share the expenses of starting and renovating your property with partners or investors and then lease the B&B from the partnership or corporation. Or you might choose to do it all yourself but to set up the business as an LLC, a limited liability corporation, to protect your own assets from any problems the B&B might incur.

If you're not a legal eagle, all this can get complicated and confusing. Take your questions to your attorney and let her help you choose the best entity for your situation.

Expert Counsel

While you won't need to call on her often, you should have an attorney who understands small-business law and is also, preferably, on the inside track in your town so if you run into difficulties with planning boards or building departments, she can help smooth your path. If you're buying or leasing an existing B&B, you may also want your attorney to look over all the paperwork both while the deal is in negotiations and before you sign on the dotted line.

Along with your accountant, your attorney should also be able to help you decide on the best structure for your business and look over any contracts, such as those with reservations services, that you may want to enter into.

You'll also want an accountant to fill out those tax returns and quarterly sales and bed tax reports, and to advise you of any special ways you can save money with your business structure.

Up with Insurance

While you're worrying about legal and accounting matters, you'll need to very carefully consider the issue of insurance. In a nutshell, you'll need it. Although the great majority of guests are nice, charming, ungreedy people, there's always the possibility that somebody can sue you in any number of horrifying scenarios, including slipping and falling on your property, choking on your breakfast, developing a life-threatening allergy to something in your house, "losing" jewelry or other valuables, or getting drunk on that sherry in the library, getting into a car, and maiming somebody.

Before you start hyperventilating, take heart. There's insurance out there to help safeguard you against all of these nightmare scenarios. If you'll be a small or homestay B&B, you might be able to persuade your homeowner's carrier to add on a few special riders. But you'll probably do far better to go with a special bed and breakfast policy. These are available—typically at discounted rates—through associations like Professional Association of Innkeepers International and various reservation services.

Beware!

Insurance companies may insist that you have antiques and other expensive fine furnishings, as well as jewelry, silver, and coins, appraised before they'll offer replacement value. And appraisers like to be paid for their efforts!

You'll want to go over policies, benefits, clauses, and riders in-depth with your insurance agent as they apply to your specific situation. The following elements will give you an idea of some issues to be aware of:

- *Personal injury*. You'll want to make sure you're covered for illness, injuries, or—worse—death of guests, guests of guests, service people, and other visitors to your inn.

- *Contents coverage*. Consider all the contents of your B&B, not just the fine antiques and historical memorabilia, but routine items like linens, TVs, kitchen equipment, and dishes, then think of how much it would cost to replace them all in the event of a fire or other disaster. You'll want to specify current replacement value, or how much it would cost to go out and buy those things now, not what they would fetch if you sold them today. (A used TV, for instance, might be worth only $30 to $50, but to properly replace it—to buy it today—might cost $150.)

- *Liability for guests' property*. This will cover you should guests' valuables become lost or damaged.

- *Liquor liability*. Coverage for guests who imbibe bubbly or other alcohol served by you and then become injured or injure someone else while under the influence.

- *Wind and flood*. In some areas of the country, especially those prone to hurricanes and tornados, you need a separate wind policy to cover buildings. In some areas, flood insurance is also a separate policy.

- *Fire*. This is generally a given in any insurance policy, but make sure you've got it and that it covers you for the current replacement value of your inn.

- *Outbuildings and signs*. Some policies automatically cover outbuildings like sheds and garages; others require a special rider. The same goes for signs, fences, and other appurtenances.

- *Loss of income.* If you have to close your doors because of fire or natural disaster, this provision makes sure you get paid some or all of the room revenues you'll lose while repairs are being made.
- *Workers' compensation.* Also a separate policy, this covers you for injury or illness of your employees.

6

The Front Desk
Your Office
Start-Up Costs

One of the biggest issues in starting your bed and breakfast is finances. How much will it cost you to get up and running? Will you be able to afford it? We'll explore all the costs involved in starting and running your B&B—as well as figuring out how much you can expect to earn—in the next three chapters. Your start-up expenses will fall into two basic categories:

1. Office and administrative expenses—everything from a computer and cell phone to membership fees for trade organizations
2. Purchase and renovation costs, and inventory items from towels and linens to housekeeping supplies

We'll explore each of these categories in a separate chapter, with this one devoted to office setup costs.

The Reservations Center

Perhaps the most important office item on your start-up list is a computer system—a hard drive, monitor, mouse, modem, and printer, plus whatever peripherals you choose to tack on. With a good system as your reservations center and office manager, you can easily—and professionally—tackle any number of B&B business tasks, including:

- Track reservations and deposits
- Perform accounting functions and generate financial reports
- Create your own brochures, display ads, and other direct-mail pieces
- Maintain guest databases
- Access research materials and other resources online
- Market your B&B online

Your new computer should be a high-quality PC. As of this writing, you can get a name-brand PC run by a Pentium-class processor with a current version of the Microsoft Vista operating system with all the short-term (RAM) and long-term memory capacity you might ever need plus a CD/DVD drive with a built-in fast modem and as well as wireless capabilities, keyboard, monitor, and reasonable quality printer/scanner/copier for pretty close to $1000.

Front Desk Fun

Your computer can make running your front desk fun, easy, and relatively goof-proof. But to do all this, it needs software. You'll find a stunning array of software lining the shelves of most office supply stores, ready to help you perform

Tip...

Smart Tip

These days, monitors are often sold separately so you can customize your computer system to whatever best suits your needs. The standard is a 15" monitor but you'll want an SVGA high-resolution color display and a screen large enough to make long-term viewing comfortable, say 17 inches and up. Remember that spending a few extra dollars upfront will save hours of squinting in the long haul. You can expect to dish out $300 to $400 for a solid, midrange model.

every business task—design and print your own checks, develop professional-quality marketing materials, make mailing lists and labels, and even do your own accounting.

Most new computers come preloaded with all the software you'll need for basic office procedures. If yours doesn't come already equipped with the following programs, shop till you drop for versions you like, then load them up:

- *Word processing programs.* You can dash off booking confirmations, contracts, press releases, and articles with a word processing program. You can even write your own B&B cookbook to sell! If you get a Microsoft-driven PC, then Microsoft Word will come with it. Corel WordPerfect can be had for under $200.

- *Accounting programs.* You can use QuickBooks or Microsoft Money to track your business finances. Virtual checkbooks, these programs allow you to track income and expenses, print out all sorts of financial reports, and even write checks. Expect to pay $49 to $199 for your cyberspace accountant.

Software Saviors

Specialized innkeeping software can be a savior and make your life far easier. With a good program, you can keep daily, weekly, and monthly reservation calendars, track deposit due dates and amounts, and set seasonal room rates and package pricing. You can compute guest billings including all applicable taxes, then print them out, and easily manage otherwise-awkward group reservations by splitting billings if necessary.

Some innkeeping programs come with availability calendars that you upload onto your web site so guests can check the dates you have open before calling to make reservations. (You might think this would discourage calls if you're already booked on their preferred dates, but it actually encourages guests to call anyway, perhaps because of the implication that you're a hot property... which then gives you the opportunity to sell them another date.)

In addition to all this, you can track your occupancy rates and inventory, write snail-mail and send e-mail reservation confirmation letters, note guests' food preferences (vegetarian, egg allergy, or whatever), and even note guests' birthdays and anniversaries for follow-up marketing.

Innkeeping software prices vary with the vendor and the number of options you choose. Expect to pay $400 to $900—check out contact information for innkeeping software vendors in the Appendix.

- *Desktop-publishing programs.* You can use these to create cards, brochures, and all sorts of other sales and promotional materials. Again, if your computer runs on the Microsoft operating system, Microsoft Publisher will probably already be installed. Another good choice is Broderbund's Print Shop Deluxe, which tallies in at about $50.

- *List-management programs.* For those mailing lists you'll develop of past and potential guests, you'll want to purchase a list management program like Parsons Technology's Ultimate Mail Manager—which includes U.S. Postal Service-certified technology for ZIP code accuracy—for about $60.

Net-cessity

By this time, you'll have realized that internet access is a must for the innkeeper. You'll need an internet service provider, or ISP, like America Online, Earthlink, or the bevy of other providers out there so you can use the web for advertising, researching, and for communicating with your guests via e-mail. Most ISPs charge about $20 to $25 per month and give you unlimited web and e-mail access.

A dial-up connection is less expensive but excruciatingly slow and comes with high rates of getting bumped off. It's worth the cost of the setup fee, the special modem, and the monthly fee for high-speed connections.

Cable connections, which operate through the same connection as the cable TV service that brings you HBO and Nickelodeon, are by far the fastest. You'll pay a setup fee of about $100, purchase a special modem for $200 to $350, and pay a monthly fee of about $50. Or you might choose to go with a DSL or ISDN connection—not quite as fast but light years ahead of the standard ISP. For these, you'll pay similar costs—setup fees of $100 to $200, terminals or modems for $200 to $250, and monthly fees of $40 to $60.

Web Basics

The ISP, however, is only part of the picture. If you'll have your own web site, you'll also need to consider its design and construction. If you're lucky enough to have a computer brain in the family, or if you take the time to become your own web expert, you can pencil in a zero under web site design and construction costs. If you outsource the task to a professional web site designer, you should ink in about $500 to $1,000. Or make arrangements with a web designer to put up your site in exchange for a weekend at your inn.

Once you've got your site up and running, you'll need a web host—an ISP-like service—to carry the site. Fees range from $30 to $50 per month for simple hosting. If you'll want a web guru to make periodic updates or changes to your site as well as host it, bump those figures up to $150 and up, depending on the complexity of the site. (This is why it behooves you to learn to do your own web design or find a friend who'll do it in exchange for your special cinnamon rolls and house coffee.)

Digitally Mastered

If you plan to produce your own web site or your own advertising materials (or both), you might want to spring for a digital camera. With one of these gadgets, you simply snap photos of your B&B exterior and guest rooms and upload the photos to your web site, your reservation service's site, or into your desktop-publishing program for manipulation into advertising materials. Expect to pay from $200 to $700 for a good-quality digital camera.

You may also want to consider buying a scanner, a keen gadget that imports or "pastes" graphics from just about any printed medium—books, photographs, brochures, or original art, for example—into your desktop-publishing program. You can pick up a print-quality scanner for about $150 to $300; and inexpensive scanner can be had in a 3-for-1 machine that includes fax and printer as well.

Print Perfection

A good printer is a must. You'll have all those confirmation letters, guest billings, press releases, promotional materials, mailing labels, and sundry other materials, and they all need to look polished and professional. Purchase an inkjet capable of producing every conceivable color as well as black and white for $200 to $1,000. One key feature to look for is a high page-per-minute rate.

The Fax of Life

Now that just about everybody communicates by e-mail, a fax machine is not a hard-and-fast necessity. But it's a nice touch, and you'll find there's always something—a vendor's order form, a scary letter from the IRS to be forwarded to your accountant, or a county pool permit form—that can't be sent the e-mail route. If you want just the fax, you can purchase a basic plain-paper model for as little as $80 or a fancy multifunctional one for up to $900.

> **Smart Tip** *Tip...*
> If you really want to impress your guest, spring for wireless internet service. Guests would then be able to bring their laptops and tap into your connection. This a good marketing tool if you are trying to attract business travelers.

Power Loss Protection

There's nothing to match the sinking sensation of losing all the data you've carefully entered into your computer, which can happen if lightning strikes your system, or even if a power surge spikes through the lines. That's why you need an uninterruptible power supply, or UPS, especially if you live in an area where thunderstorms or power surges are common. Instead of losing power to your system—and all your data—when the house power fails or flickers, the unit flashes switches your power to its short-term battery and flashes red and sounds a warning, giving you ample time to safely shut down.

If you link to the internet through the telephone, you want to be sure that your UPS includes phone line protection for any surges coming in through the telephone wires. Expect to pay $150 and up.

Surge Safety

A surge protector safeguards your other electronic equipment from power spikes during storms and outages. Your UPS will double as a surge protector for your computer hard drive, or CPU, and monitor, but you'll want protection for those other valuable office allies—your printer, fax machine, and copier. They don't need a battery backup because no data will be lost if the power goes out, and a surge protector will do the job for a lot less money. If you've got a fax machine, be sure the surge protector also defends its phone line. Expect to pay in the range of $15 to $60.

The Phone Connection

As a B&B host, your phone—along with your computer—will be your staunchest ally, the instrument that brings you those reservations! So you'll want two separate, dedicated lines for your inn: one for handling phone calls and another for your fax machine and ISP. If you've ever tried to call a friend who's got his phone line tied up surfing the internet and gotten a seemingly endless busy signal, you'll know how important this is. You simply can't let phone calls go unanswered—it's not only unprofessional but results in lost reservations. If potential guests can't reach you, they'll call another inn.

Costs vary with the number of features you add to your telephone service, and which local and long-distance carriers you go with. For the

> **Tip...**
>
> ### Smart Tip
> The copier is an optional item, but as you grow you may find it necessary for running off forms, fliers, and other goodies. It's far easier to run off one copy or 50 in your own office than to have to run down to the copy center every time the need arises. Copiers range from $200 to $1,000 and up.

purposes of start-up budgeting, let's say you should allocate about $40 per line. You'll also need to add the phone company's installation fee, which should be in the range of $40 to $60. Check with your local phone company to determine exactly what these costs are in your area.

Keep in mind, too, that these lines will be for B&B business only. You'll want to keep your home line separate so the kids, if they don't have their own cell phones, can jabber away to their friends without interrupting inn business.

Telephonics

Because it's so important not to miss calls from prospective guests, you'll want a cordless phone that you can carry with you from room to room—and even out into the garden. These come in single- and two-line versions. If you choose the latter, you can have your office line on one and your home line on the other with a hold button to switch between calls if necessary.

A speaker is a nice feature for your two-line phone, especially for all those on-hold forever calls to your banker, attorney, insurance company, or whoever. Your hands are free and there's no earring jabbing you in the side of the head while you listen to canned Perry Como favorites.

Expect to pay $150–$200 for a two-line speaker phone with auto redial, memory dial, flashing lights, mute button, and other assorted goodies. Shoot for a phone with a power range of at least 900 MHz and preferably 2.4GHz; the higher the range, the further from the base you can wander with the handset.

Going Cellular

Since your phone will be your lifeline, you'll also want to spring for a cellular phone. Then, instead of missing calls while you're out running errands, you can forward your business line to your cell phone and take reservations—or guests' phone numbers so you can get back to them—while standing in line at the bank or in the frozen foods section of the supermarket. "We transfer our phone to our cellular so we're always in contact with prospective guests," says Marilyn Lewis in Fort Worth, Texas. "You have to always answer your phone—you have to catch people when they call, or they'll go to someone else."

The cellular phone market, like that of just about every other electronic gizmo currently available, changes with the speed of light, with

> **Tip...**
>
> ### Smart Tip
> When you get that cellular phone, you'll also need an extra battery and a cord to connect the phone to the power outlet (formerly the cigarette lighter) of your car. These are extras and go for $20 to $50 for a battery and $15 to $25 for the cord.

new models available all the time. Because the market is so competitive, new pricing plans are always coming online as well.

Evaluate as carefully as possible the times you'll most need your cellular phone. Will you run most of your errands on weekends or after 7 in the evening? (Many plans offer free weekends and weeknights.) If you'll be out during weekdays, about how often and for how long? Do you expect most of your calls to be incoming or will you also need to make outgoing calls, for instance, checking in with your spouse or parent or whoever may be minding the inn?

Cell phone payment plans are based on the number of minutes you're using the phone—some charge for both incoming and outgoing calls, some for outgoing only. Either way, those minutes add up faster than you might imagine. Choose the plan that seems best for you. Most service providers will allow you to change plans if your current one doesn't suit, but most will also lock you into a one-year contract. So shop around. Your location may limit the number of cell phone companies you have access to.

As for the phone itself, models are getting smaller and more high-tech all the time. Providers will often give you a phone (usually a model that's just become outdated) for free when you sign up. This phone will probably do fine—you don't need anything particularly fancy. If you want to, or must choose, go for a model that's small enough to tuck into a pocket or purse but weighty enough to hold a battery charge for at least two days.

The Virtual Receptionist

Even with cordless and cellular phones at the ready, you'll still need a virtual receptionist to answer the phone after hours or while you're at the dentist. Your choices are voice mail or a good old-fashioned answering machine.

Like an answering machine, voice mail takes your messages when you're not in the office. If you have call waiting, a feature which discreetly beeps to announce an incoming call while you're already on the phone, and you choose not to answer that second call, voice mail will take a message for you. With voice mail, as with many answering machines, you can access your messages from a remote location.

Voice mail costs depend on your local phone company and the features you choose, but you can expect to pay in the range of $6 to $20 a month. Answering machines run from $40 to $150, depending on the features you opt for.

Phones range from $100 for an average-size model to $500 for the top-of-the-line, super-small model. Monthly fees can range from $40 to $150 or more, depending on the plan, the service provider, and the competition in your area.

Charge It!

If you'll start off with a homestay or small B&B, you may not want to take credit cards—guests will cheerfully pay by cash or check. But for the larger inn—and even for the homestay—taking credit cards makes you much more appealing to guests. They don't have to consult their bank balance before making reservations; they can charge their stay. So you'll probably want to invest in an electronic credit card terminal.

More and more merchant card service firms cater specifically to the SOHO (small office/home office) entrepreneur, and that includes the B&B host. Shop around (especially on the web), and you'll find a variety to choose from.

What can you expect to pay for an electronic terminal? Fees depend on several factors, including the company you go with and your personal credit history. You can lease or purchase the terminal itself from the merchant bank, or you can buy a used (but still serviceable) machine from a company that's gone out of business or has upgraded its unit. Take a look at the "Electronic Card Fees" chart on page 100 for more information.

> ### Smart Tip
> Tip...
>
> If you sign up with a reservations service, you pay a yearly fee of $15 to $75—don't forget to add it into your start-up costs.

The Meter Maid

If you plan on sending out a lot of direct-mail pieces, a postage meter may keep you from going postal. Depending on how spiffy you choose to go from among the various models available, you cannot only stamp your mail but fold, staple, insert, seal, label, weigh, sort, stack, and wrap it. And where you once had to lug your postage meter down to the post office and stand in line to get it reset, you don't any more. Now you simply reset via phone or computer.

The fancier and faster the machine, the more expensive it will be to rent, lease, or purchase. As a ballpark figure, you can expect to rent a simple—and adequate—postage meter/electronic scale combo for about $30 per month and up.

Office Furnishings

Your office should be tucked away in your private quarters (or in a larger inn, in a separate room behind a locked door), out of sight from possible prying eyes. Since guests won't see it, you don't need anything fancy in the way of office furniture. But you will need something to sit on and something to hold your computer equipment and files. Expect to find midrange desks from $200 to $600, computer work centers for $200, chairs from $60 to $280, printer stands from $50 to $75, two-drawer, letter-size file cabinets (which can double as your printer stand) from $30 to $100, and four-shelf bookcases for $70.

Office Supplies

Your computer and printer won't do much good without paper on which to process your work. You'll also need to round out your office supplies with stationery, envelopes, business cards, pens, pencils, and all those miscellaneous bits such as paper clips, tape, and staples.

Plan on allocating about $25 to $50 for a box of good-quality printer/copier paper, which will give you ten reams of 500 sheets each. You'll spend in the range of $200 to $400 for stationery, printed at a quick-stop place like Kinko's.

Grand Open House

Kick off the formal inauguration of your new B&B with a festive grand opening. Invite friends, family, suppliers, folks on your mailing list, and local news media. Match your event to the theme and ambience of your inn. Make it an elegant evening soiree for an elegant townhouse, a garden tea for a B&B with lush gardens for guests to enjoy, an evening of Edwardian society for a historic Edwardian mansion, or a Key West-type sunset celebration for a casual beach house.

Have each party-goer sign a guest book that includes space for addresses, which will give you names for your mailing list. Hand out brochures and rate sheets and perhaps a small giveaway like an herbal sachet or bookmark imprinted with your logo.

Members of the Club

We've now given you a shopping list of every item for the well-equipped B&B front desk and back office—including two take-along checklists to have in hand when you hit the office and computer superstores. (You'll find them below.)

But there's more. Don't forget to budget for membership in professional organizations—besides help in starting and growing your business, these groups give members discounts on all sorts of business services, help you stay up to speed on industry issues and events, and act as your voice in legislative affairs. Annual fees typically range from $95 to $200.

Plugging In/Adding Up

OK, now it's time to don your bookkeeping cap and tally up the company start-up expenses we've investigated in this chapter. Besides the ones we've already checked into, you'll want to add other expenses like business licenses, business insurance, legal advice, and all the other costs intrinsic to any company's birth. And don't forget to throw in a grand opening celebration!

To give you an idea of how much you can expect to budget, check out the "Estimated Company Start-Up Costs" on page 97 for two hypothetical bed and

Office Supplies Mini-Shopping List

Computer/copier/fax paper	$_____
Blank business cards	_____
Blank letterhead stationery	_____
Matching envelopes	_____
File folders	_____
Return address stamp or stickers	_____
Extra printer cartridge	_____
Mouse pad	_____
Miscellaneous office supplies (pencils, paper clips, etc.)	_____
Extra fax cartridge	_____
Total Costs	$_____

Office Equipment Checklist

Use this handy list as a shopping guide for equipping your front desk and office. It's been designed with the one-person office in mind, so if you've got partners, employees, or you just won $250,000 in merchandise from an office supplies superstore, you may want to make modifications.

After you've finished your shopping, fill in the purchase price next to each item, add up the total, and use this figure in the "Company Start-Up Costs Worksheet" on page 98.

❑ Current Windows-based Pentium-class PC with
   SVGA monitor, modem, and CD-ROM $ _____

❑ Inkjet printer   _____

❑ Fax machine   _____

❑ Software:
   innkeeping   _____
   word processing   _____
   desktop publishing   _____
   accounting   _____
   list management   _____

❑ Phones, two to three lines with voice mail, or   _____

❑ Answering machine   _____

❑ Cellular phone   _____

❑ Uninterruptible power supply   _____

❑ Surge protector   _____

❑ Calculator   _____

❑ Office supplies (see the mini-list on page 95)   _____

Not on the critical list:

❑ Digital camera   _____

❑ Scanner   _____

❑ Copier   _____

❑ Desk   _____

❑ Desk chair   _____

❑ Filing cabinet   _____

❑ Bookcase   _____

Total Costs $ _____

breakfasts, Pieces of Eight B&B and Lightning Bug Bay B&B. Pieces of Eight will offer four guest rooms in the owners' present seaside five-bedroom, three-bath home, to which they'll add two new bathrooms. Lightning Bug Bay will offer eight guest rooms, six in a rustic house overlooking a lake and two in an adjoining carriage house. Its owners will purchase and renovate the property.

The smaller inn will operate with its two owners—a recently retired couple—as the sole employees. They already have a computer system and software and don't plan to upgrade in the near future. The larger inn's owners have fled the rat race, although the wife will do homebased consulting work while they build the B&B business. They plan to hire one employee and also plan to start off with all-new, top-of-the-line equipment.

Estimated Company Start-Up Costs

Costs	Pieces of Eight	Lightning Bug Bay
Professional associations	$375	$575
Office equipment (see chart on page 96)	1,537	5,915
Licenses	200	300
Phone	180	240
Magazine subscriptions	56	56
Grand opening	200	500
Legal services	375	375
Miscellaneous postage	50	50
Internet service provider	300	300
Web site design and marketing	0	500
Insurance	800	1,200
Subtotal	$4,073	$10,011
Miscellaneous expenses (add 10% of total)	$407	$1,001
Total Start-Up Costs	**$4,480**	**$11,012**

97

Use the worksheet below to list your own company start-up costs. If you copy a couple of extra sheets, you can work up several options, compare them all, and decide which will be the best for you.

Company Start-Up Costs Worksheet

Professional associations $ _____

Office equipment
    (see chart on page 96)   _____

Licenses   _____

Phone   _____

Magazine subscriptions   _____

Grand opening   _____

Legal services   _____

Miscellaneous postage   _____

Internet service provider   _____

Web site design and marketing   _____

Insurance   _____

Subtotal $ _____

Miscellaneous expenses
    (add 10% of total)   _____

Your Total Start-Up Costs $ _____

Office Equipment and Supplies Costs

Furniture, Equipment, and Supplies	Pieces of Eight	Lightning Bug Bay
Professional associations	$375	$575
Computer system (including printer)	0	1,500
Fax machine	250	350
Software	300	500
Cordless two-line phone	200	200
Cellular phone	100	100
Uninterruptible power supply	125	125
Surge protector	34	34
Calculator	50	50
Postage meter	30	50
Copier	0	500
Electronic credit card terminal	0	450
Desk	0	200
Desk chair	0	60
Printer stand	0	50
File cabinet	0	50
Bookcase	0	70
Printer/copier paper	25	50
Stationery	200	300
#10 blank envelopes	3	6
Address stamp or stickers	10	10
Extra printer cartridges	70	70
Extra fax cartridge	80	80
Mouse pad	10	10
Miscellaneous office supplies	50	100
Total Costs	**$1,912**	**$5,490**

Electronic Card Fees

Item	Fees (Swiped*)	Fees (Mail, Phone or Internet Order)
Discount Rate (multiply each transaction by this rate, e.g., $200 ticket fee x 1.59% = $3.18 that the bank charges you to process the transaction)	1.50% to 1.59%	2.09% to 2.50%
Transaction Fee (another fee the bank adds on for each transaction processed)	$0.20	$0.25 to $0.30
Monthly Statement Fee	$5 to $10	$5 to $15
Monthly Minimum (if your monthly sales are less than a specified amount, you pay this amount)	$10 to $20	$10 to $20
Application Fee	$0 to $75	$0 to $75
Progamming Fee	usually free with equipment lease or purchase	usually free with equipment lease or purchase
Electronic Card	$300 to $600 purchase	$300 to $600 purchase
Terminal	$19 to $21/mo. lease option	$19 to $62/mo. lease option

*Merchant card services charge higher discount rates for orders taken by mail, internet or phone than for those handled in person or swiped through the credit card terminal. Why? Because if a customer signs the credit card bill while standing there, you and the merchant service run less risk of a charge-back.

**In addition to the fees shown here, you may be charged an AVF or address verification fee per transaction, a daily batchout fee to send charges from the electronic terminal to the merchant service in batches or chunks, and an annual "membership" fee. Be sure to ask—and negotiate—before you sign up!

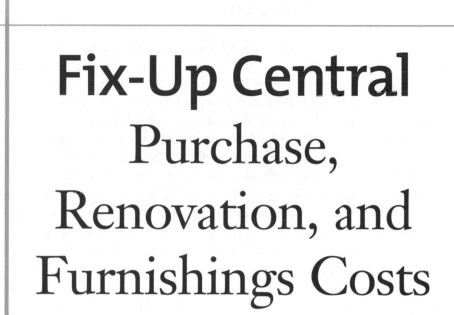

7

Fix-Up Central
Purchase, Renovation, and Furnishings Costs

For many aspiring innkeepers, buying the perfect property and fixing it up is at least half the fun. If this is you, read on. Even if you buy an existing B&B or use your present digs, you may still need to remodel, redecorate, or add upgrades like in-room fireplaces or whirlpool tubs. In this chapter, we'll explore the costs of purchasing, renovating, and decorating as well as of setting up bed and breakfast housekeeping with furnishings and supplies.

Buying the Dream

While we can give you a fair estimate of how much you'll pay for a computer system, a ream of copier paper, and a cellular phone, it would be impossible to tell you how much you'll pay for the house you'll transform into your dream B&B. Property prices vary dramatically, not only from state to state and region to region but even from neighborhood to neighborhood within the same city. And two homes of the same size and floor plan on the same street can sell for entirely different prices depending on the upgrades of one or the neglect of the other or on how badly a particular buyer wants out of an existing mortgage, due to divorce, death in the family, or career transfer.

So our objective here is to give you the tools to determine for yourself how much the various homes you'll view will cost, then to choose the one that makes your heart sing.

Our hypothetical innkeepers, whom you briefly met in Chapter 6, have kindly offered their own properties as examples. Read through this chapter, and then take a look at their line-item costs laid out in the form on page 124. As you'll recall, Pieces of Eight's owners will convert their existing home by adding two bathrooms. Lightning Bug Bay's owners, on the other hand, will purchase a house and then renovate it to B&B standards. So let's take a look at their process.

Mountain High

Lightning Bug's owners chose to relocate from the city to the mountains—they'd vacationed in the area for years and fallen in love with the tranquility, the sweeping vistas and, of course, the lightning bugs. When they decided to make their move, they chose to focus their house search on areas they knew from their market research were popular tourist destinations. This, they felt, would increase their chances of occupancy rate success even though they'd be the new kids on the block.

After viewing dozens of potential properties, they chose a six-bedroom, three-bath home that has two large rooms with attached baths over the garage. Originally built in 1934 as a Chicago tycoon's summer cottage, the house had been sold several times over the years, and then fallen into disrepair. The bathrooms were remodeled in 1962 by someone with more perspiration than inspiration, and the house had been occupied only sporadically since then as a family getaway.

The home was listed at $395,000 but had been on the market for almost a year. When our buyers came along with an offer of $379,000—pointing out the many costs involved in returning the house to livable condition—the sellers accepted.

The Cost of Buying

But the future Lightning Bug Bay B&B is going to cost its ecstatic new owners considerably more than that terrifically negotiated price of $379,000. Before they've even signed the final papers, they'll have to spring for all sorts of purchase-related expenses.

First they'll have to come up with the down payment, which is usually 20 percent of the purchase price, although it can be as low as 5 percent or as high as 25 percent. Here, it's 20 percent, or $75,800. Of course, the down payment is actually part of the purchase price and not a tacked-on fee, but it is something you'll have to come up with right away.

Then there are the closing costs, of which there always seem to be an inordinate number. The following items are the highlights, says Rick Casey of Bay Properties in Panama City Beach, Florida, although there are lots more as you'll see from the following closing costs estimates.

- *Appraisal.* As we explored in Chapter 4, banks won't lend money on the property unless it appraises for at least the sales price—or unless you can make other creative arrangements.

- *Survey.* The bank will want to see a survey—one that shows the property's boundaries in relation to neighboring properties, roads and easements, and also marks the location of structures on the property itself. If the survey shows the house you're buying has, say, three feet of garage on your neighbor's land, the problem will have to be corrected before they'll sign over the mortgage.

- *Loan origination fee.* This is a percentage of the loan amount you'll pay upfront for the privilege of being granted a mortgage. Not all banks charge these fees; if your bank does, don't hesitate to try to negotiate it lower. If you do pay, expect costs of .5 percent to 3 percent of the loan amount.

- *Title insurance.* The title company does a search of the title and deed of the property, checking for any problems that might invalidate your right to the property after purchase. These include horror-scenario things like the house being sold sometime in the past to someone other than the current seller who failed to record the deed but suddenly shows up with it, or a contractor or creditor turning up with a lien on the house. When the search turns up nothing, the title company then provides you with

> **Stat Fact**
> The bank will require you to have homeowner's insurance on the property before closing the sale and assigning you the mortgage. You'll want it, too, as well as the other types of coverage we explored in Chapter 5.

insurance against any such horror coming to light at a later date. Banks won't lend money if there's no title insurance on the property.

- *Recording fees and stamps.* Everybody wants a piece of the pie. These are miscellaneous dribs and drabs of fees charged by your city, county, and/or state. They can range from $25 to $500 or more, depending on the purchase price and local rates. You should also count in another $50 to $100 or more for sundry other fees, from FedEx charges to bank processing fees.

Back to the Future

Once all the paperwork is over and the house is yours, how much will it cost to bring it back to its glorified past while updating it and taking it into the future? Again, your renovation costs are entirely dependent on your particular circumstances. A 100-year-old fixer only Bob Vila could love will cost a lot more to restore than a 30-year-young house that only needs new paint and flooring to bring it from the Age of Aquarius into the new millennium.

Lightning Bug Bay will create three new bathrooms in the main house, one from an existing closet and two from an existing library. They'll also rejuvenate the three bathrooms in the main house as well as the two bathrooms in the apartments over the garage (soon to become suites), and generally spruce up the entire property with paint and wallpaper. The new owners love the original hardwood floors, which will need to be refinished, and the old-fashioned kitchen, which will get new appliances and new countertops. At some point in the future, the owners plan to convert the garage into cozy quarters for themselves. For now, however, they'll live in the main house while they remodel.

Taking a Bath

To estimate the costs for all this, they'll need to take stock of the house's layout. Bathrooms cost more when plumbing has to be run from existing sources through several dozen feet of wall or crawl space to the new bathroom. But if you can design your spaces so the new room is back-to-back or directly above or below the existing bath, you'll save considerably. The same holds true for kitchens.

Lightning Bug's owners will also need to consider how fancy they want to go. If their goal is a standard bathroom with a shower over the tub, they'll pay considerably less than if they go for a whirlpool tub for two (or even one) and a separate shower stall with three spray heads at different heights.

Depending on which of these routes you go, you can expect to pay in the range of $7,000 to $15,000 per new bathroom, including a professional plumber and an electrician to install GFIs, or ground-fault interrupters, special outlets that help prevent accidental electrocution. If you're a handy Dan or Anne and you can legally do the work yourself, you'll save considerably on these figures.

The old bathrooms have pedestal sinks, nice, deep cast-iron tubs, and ceramic tile on the floors and halfway up the walls. The owners will scrape and regrout the tile, update the faucets and towel bars, but otherwise keep the rooms in their original style—even, as much as possible, the new downstairs unit that will be wheelchair-accessible. The new bathrooms will be done with ceramic tile floors, whirlpool tubs, pedestal sinks, and period fixtures to match the rest of the house. Cost to upgrade five existing bathrooms: $2,500. Cost to create three new bathrooms: $45,000.

Sprucing Up

Lightning Bug's owners will tackle the painting on their own, so they'll save on labor costs. Which is good, because before they can paint they'll have to scrape and sand the woodwork as well as remove some astonishingly unattractive old wallpaper. They plan to spend about $5,000 on interior paint.

You can go one of two routes to determine your own painting costs: 1) get bids from reputable paint contractors, or 2) figure it out—and do the work—yourself. One gallon of paint covers about 400 square feet. Paint prices vary from $8 to $33 per gallon, depending on the quality, the store, and whether you go for Wal-Mart's best or Ralph Lauren's.

After the owners got bids on refinishing and varnishing the hardwood floors—and after the smelling salts kicked in—they decided to add this job to the list of projects they'll do themselves, at a fraction of the cost. They can rent a heavy-duty floor sander and purchase varnish for under $500. Hiring a professional would cost just over $5,000.

If you choose to do it yourself, you can figure one gallon of varnish for every 250 square feet of thirsty wood flooring. Or plan to hire a professional floor refinisher who'll charge about $1.75 to $2 per square foot.

Cleaning Up In the Kitchen

Lightning Bug's owners will update the sunny, old-fashioned kitchen by purchasing a new range, refrigerator, and dishwasher. They'll also replace the old, chipped

▲

Warm and Cozy

Since the Lightning Bug house was built in 1934, it doesn't have much in the way of heating and air conditioning except wood-burning fireplaces in the common rooms and the living areas of the above-garage units. The owners have sprung for a central system for the common rooms and kitchen at a cost of about $5,000. They'll put gas fireplaces in each guest room for heat; since they're in the mountains, they'll let open windows provide cool night breezes. Cost: $650 per unit.

Most old homes aren't insulated well, if at all. Since the house was built as a summer residence, it's lacking in this department. The owners will open the inside of all guest room exterior walls and one side of each interior wall and have their electrician run wire for phone and cable as well as install new electrical, phone and cable outlets. (He'll also wire and add outlets to common rooms.) The owners will then cover the insulation with new fire-rated drywall. Cost for insulation and drywall materials: $4,000. Cost for electrician, wiring, and outlets: $2,000.

---

ceramic tile counters with new tile that will retain the same look. The old, stained sink will go out, to be replaced with a new cast-iron one for which they'll pay $200, a new faucet for $150, and a new garbage disposal for $100. They'll pay about $1,200 for the fridge, $1,200 for a top-of-the-line range and hood, and $500 for a dishwasher.

The tile contractor who'll do the bathrooms will also install the counters and set the sink. Cost for the job, including labor and materials: $700. The electrician who does the bathrooms will install extra outlets above the counters and add overhead lighting. The cost for this, including labor and light fixtures, tallies in at $400.

Total cost for the kitchen project: $4,450.

And Such As That

Lightning Bug's owners will spring for two heavy-duty stackable washer/dryer units for $1,250 each. Their plumber will install a new 40-gallon high-recovery water heater, priced at $300, next to the existing one and tie them together. A private telephone company will install a hotel-style system that will provide service to each guest room. An auto-attendant will answer the phone (so the owners don't have to play switchboard operator) and will track outgoing toll calls, which will be added to guests' bills. The cost: $2,500 for the system itself, plus a one-time fee of $30 per line.

Smart Tip

Adding insulation to walls not only helps with heating and cooling bills but adds all-important sound insulation as well, which your guest will thank you for!

Tip...

In addition to all this, each bedroom will receive a new master-keyed locking door knob, and exterior doors will be graced with new locks and hardware. As well, they'll install hard-wired smoke detectors and ceiling fan/light fixtures to each guest room as well as in other areas of the house. Total cost for all these miscellaneous, but definitely important, extras including labor: $7,420.

Outside Spiffing

Moving outside, the owners will tackle the exterior painting on their own, spending about $15,000 on materials. The home's roof and gutter system are fine, as are its wide, perfect-for-rocking-chairs, porches.

They'll add a gravel parking pad onto the existing sweeping driveway and install lights along the parking area and walkways. They'll do the landscaping themselves, including tuning up the existing watering system. And they'll commission a discreet sign on the lawn, at $150, to which the electrician will run a line for a discreet light. Total cost including labor: $3,650.

Love and Panic

As you can see, renovating an old home requires as much bank balance (or loan) as brains and brawn. Fun, creative, and intensely rewarding, yes. Inexpensive, no. Our hypothetical innkeepers will spend nearly $100,000 on remodeling alone. They haven't yet touched on the costs of furnishing and supplying their B&B.

And while Lightning Bug Bay is definitely a "This Old House" candidate, it's been a fairly simple remodel. It's in good condition structurally and because of its no-frills lodge look, it doesn't have all the gingerbread, scrollwork, and wood-and-plaster ornamentation that many older historic homes are famous for. Its owners haven't had to touch the roof or foundation or make any structural repairs. They haven't needed to replaster old walls and, except for their hardwood floors, they haven't had to

Smart Tip

Save time and money by purchasing a good quality paint, in the $15 to $20 range. Cheap paint won't cover well or last long and is not washable—you'll end up repainting either immediately or in the near future.

Tip...

Smart Tip

Tip...

Always factor into your budget 10 percent over your estimated remodeling costs to cover the unexpected that's sure to come up.

spend (or pay someone else to spend) countless hours stripping, painting, and restoring old woodwork.

It can be so effortless to fall in love with an old home that you overlook its blemishes. You don't realize the extent of the work involved until you get into it—and panic sets in. And remember, you've got to consider not only the actual restoration that will bring it back to its former beauty but also the costs of bringing it into the modern age.

Old homes often have eccentric and unsafe electrical wiring and only one or a few outlets per room, which was fine when there were few electrical appliances. But when you've got an electric range, range hood, refrigerator, dishwasher, garbage, disposal, toaster, coffee maker, food processor, can opener, and cordless phone—and perhaps more gadgets—all demanding power at the same time in just one room, you'll need more juice and more outlets. Guest rooms and bathrooms will require places to plug in electric shavers, hair dryers, curling irons, laptop computers, reading lamps, TVs, vacuum cleaners, and carpet shampooers. Your office will need outlets and phone jacks to accommodate your computer, printer, modem, fax machine, copier, desk lamp, phone, and calculator. You'll also want to bring your historic home up to date with wiring for cable TV service.

To help you get a grip on the extent of renovations before you get started—before you even purchase the house—use the "Renovation Checklist" on page 118. Make copies for each house you get serious about, then bring the list on your handy clipboard or notebook, and scribble away. If you're not sure about an item, don't guess—consult a pro.

Updating the Homestay

Our other hypothetical B&B, as you'll recall, is Pieces of Eight, which will operate four guest rooms in the owner's present seaside five-bedroom, three-bath home. Aside from some redecorating—transforming former teens' lairs into guest havens—the only change these owners have to worry about is adding two new bathrooms, which they'll create from walk-in closets in the bedrooms.

Pieces of Eight's owners expect to spend about $10,000 per new bathroom, which will

Smart Tip

Tip...

Get project estimators and job calculators at www.improvenet.com. These cool tools will help you figure out everything from how many tiles you'll need for the bathroom floor to how much that new kitchen will cost.

include the services of a professional plumber and an electrician. Like Lightning Bug Bay's owners, they'll tackle painting the new bathrooms and the kids' bedrooms themselves and have budgeted about $500. They'll replace the old carpet and pad with new high-quality coverings at $3,000.

They'll add master-keyed new door hardware with locks and deadbolts to the guest rooms, at a cost of about $115. Instead of in-room phones, they'll add an extra line to their existing phone service, with a phone for guests' use in the study. This line will be restricted to local calls—guests will need to use a credit card to place toll calls. Cost: $60 for installation.

The owners will pave over part of their front yard to add additional parking and add tubs of flowers to compensate for downsizing the greenery. Cost: $2,300.

Total cost of renovations, not including furnishings and supplies: $25,975.

The Fun of Furnishing

You've tackled the nitty-gritty of renovations and prepped your bed and breakfast into peak physical condition: The roof is sound and the foundation solid. You've got the proper number of bathrooms, a kitchen a health inspector will love, and enough electrical, phone, and cable wiring to reach from Sarasota, Florida, to Saratoga Springs, New York.

Now comes the fun of furnishing your new inn. Whether you're starting from scratch with nothing but bare walls and floors, you've been carefully collecting period antiques for decades, or you're simply going to open a couple of bedrooms to homestay guests, you'll need to add a certain number of furnishings and housekeeping supplies to your inventory.

Your B&B should reflect your personality and your unique vision of the perfect inn—individuality is the essence of the bed and breakfast experience. But you'll also want to follow the tried-and-true guidelines of what guests expect and what innkeepers have found works best. In this section, we'll explore these items and offer tips on giving them your own stamp. You can then use the "Furnishings Checklist" on page 121 for your own furnishings countdown.

Porches and Verandas

The ambience of your B&B is set before guests even walk through the doors. If your house boasts a grand old porch or veranda, you'll want to set out rockers or a

Toy Story

If you're at the beach or in a ski area, consider how you'll handle guests' sand and snow toys. You don't want people dragging sand-encrusted floats, pails, masks and flippers, sundry, inflatables, and soon-to-be-smelly shells (and they'll bring back a lot of this stuff) into the house. But you don't want all that clutter on the porch, either. And what will you do with guests' skis, boots, poles, hiking gear, and bicycles?

Consider out-of-the-way but accessible storage, perhaps on the back porch or tucked behind the fence in your side yard. Design a space that's secure, out-of-sight and organized. You may even want to supply a small freezer in which guests can stock the fruits of fishing expeditions or an outdoor shower for rinsing off gear and guests.

swing or glider for enjoying those balmy summer nights, listening to cricket serenades and watching the world go by. You might also consider a few tables and chairs for breakfasting alfresco, playing cards, or sipping iced teas on lazy afternoons.

These furnishings should be sturdy and weather-hardy. Choose with an eye to mildew or mold on cushions and rust on metal furniture. Keep in mind that whatever you go with will probably have to be repainted every year to two years and wiped down after every morning dew or evening rain. Clean lines are the easiest to keep up; frilly pieces with lots of entwined metal leaves and flowers will require a lot more work.

Common Areas

Beyond the front door, your parlor, living room or drawing room will set the tone of your B&B for new guests. If you'll run a larger inn, you may opt for a formal "front desk" counter like those found in hotels. Chances are, however, you'll want to keep your operations homier and friendlier. So how will you check in guests? Some B&Bs feature a writing desk and a few chairs set off to one side where you and your guests can conduct paperwork. Other innkeepers choose to do all the check-in stuff in their own private office area, so there's no front desk at all.

Smart Tip

Tip...

Place your seating in friendly groups: a few chairs pulled up in front of the fire, a loveseat and sofa placed around the coffee table, or a cozy orchestration of armchairs in front of the bay window. These sorts of arrangements are more conducive to warmth and conversation than furniture antisocially pushed up against walls.

The Little Things

While guests can be wowed by a king-size bed or whirlpool tub, it's the little things that captivate them just as much. Stock bookcases with lots of reading material—those hardcover book club selections you've already read, the paperback romances you couldn't resist at the supermarket, and the *Nancy Drew* or *Babysitters Club* entries your kids outgrew but couldn't bear to throw out. You can pick up scads of nearly new books for a song at garage sales and flea markets. And it's fun to artfully scatter a few books from your historic home's heyday on coffee or side tables.

Guests also appreciate sheaves of recent-vintage magazines for whiling away the hours. Set out a variety—glam issues like *Vogue* and *Elle*, regional publications like *Southern Living* and *Yankee*, as well as *Ladies' Home Journal* and *Sports Illustrated*.

And don't forget games. Stock shelves or cupboards with packs of playing cards and checkers, chess, and Chinese checkers sets. Guests also appreciate board games. Old standbys like Monopoly and Life can seem boring at home, but placed in a vacation setting, they take on a delightfully nostalgic tone, especially when families or groups of friends are gathered. Search out "new" games of all sorts at garage sales and flea markets—but check to make sure all the pieces are intact before purchasing.

You might still want that writing desk in the corner—guests can use it to dash off postcards, scribble in diaries, or pen that birthday card to Aunt Fran. As well, you'll want seating that's adequate for the number of guests you expect. Most Americans are uncomfortable sitting hip to hip with strangers, so even though you've got a sofa that seats four, it probably won't be occupied by more than two or, in a pinch, three people at a time. Which means you'll also need a loveseat, some cushy armchairs, and a few of Sherlock Holmes' favorite, the wingback—or whatever suits your inn's style.

You'll also want a coffee table and a selection of side tables for guests to set drinks and books on. And if you have the space, a table and chairs for playing cards, or board games is a nice

Smart Tip

Tip...

Set out coasters—lots of coasters—on coffee tables, side tables, and even nightstands, anyplace guests are likely to set hot or cold drinks. A selection of whimsical or elegant styles at hand keeps guests mindful of fine furnishings.

touch. Add plenty of reading lamps so guests don't have to squint at the pages of the latest thriller or period novel from your library, as well as a selection of accent lamps to throw warm pools of light on dark nights.

For the foyer or entry hall, a hat or coat rack is a thoughtful touch, as is an umbrella stand and a mirror so guests can make that last-minute lipstick check or necktie adjustment before going out to meet friends or business acquaintances.

Smart Tip

Many innkeepers charge an additional fee, typically $20 to $25 per night, for providing a rollaway bed or cot.

Into the Bedroom

OK, you've got guest bedrooms—you'll furnish them with beds. That's a given. But the size and style will require some thought. Most people consider the king-size bed a luxury furnishing and are thrilled to get a room that contains one. It's a definite draw that will help bump up your room rates. On the other hand, a cozy Victorian chamber with smaller-scale Victorian furnishings—or any small bedroom—may be overwhelmed by a huge king bed. If you don't furnish kings, you should do your utmost to provide queens.

Then there's the issue of those few people who don't want a king bed, or any bed for two. Single girlfriends, for instance, who'll want to share a room to save money

Extra Extras

Miscellaneous extras to have on hand in each guest room include a flashlight (with live batteries) tucked into a nightstand drawer or wardrobe, a water pitcher or carafe and two glasses on a small tray, a box of tissues, and a wastebasket. If you allow smoking, you'll definitely want to add an ashtray or two. If you'll have shared baths, you'll need a towel rack.

You'll also, of course, want plenty of decorator items from prints on the walls to knickknacks to fresh-cut or silk flowers, as well as whatever else suits your inn's style and ambience. These things are important—they give the room dimension and character and lift it from the mundane to the unique. Don't be afraid to add a few touches of whimsy if they fit, like a small teddy bear perched on a shelf, a vintage sand pail on a dresser, or a fanciful print above the bed—these are the things guests remember and share with other potential guests.

Dollar Stretcher

In place of expensive night-stands, you can purchase particle board decorator tables and floor-length skirts to dress them up for about $15. You'll find them at discount stores.

may not want to get as cozy as sharing a bed. There's the rare married couple who sleeps in twin beds à la Lucy and Ricky, and the siblings or parent and child who may want the same room but not the same bed.

One obvious way to accommodate these people is to furnish one guest room with twin beds. You can transform these into a double when required by pushing the beds together and then placing a purpose-made plastic strip across the "seam" where they meet. You can also forgo the twins altogether and provide a rollaway bed for these guests, furnish one room with a daybed that offers nighttime sleeping accommodation, or offer a suite with a sofa bed in the sitting room area.

Once you've got the beds, it goes without saying that you've also got mattresses and box springs. These need to be firm but comfortable as well as sturdy. If you'll use family furnishings already on hand, lie on your beds, and pretend you're in a luxury hotel. Would you pay for a night on those mattresses? If they've been in service since Gramps was a newlywed and sag in the middle or list to one side, or your kids have used them as trampolines, it's time for a change.

Make guests comfortable with a nightstand on each side of the bed and a comfortable reading light, either one for each nightstand or one or two mounted above the bed. An alarm clock is also a nice touch so guests can rouse themselves for that 5 A.M. fishing trip or 8 A.M. business meeting.

Each guest room should have at least one armchair or straight chair (preferably two), or if space and your decor allows, a sofa or loveseat. If you have the space, a small writing desk is a nice touch. And if you plan to serve in-room breakfasts or other meals, you'll want a small table as well. Lighting is also important. You should have a ceiling fan/overhead light in each room; also consider strategic lamps for chairs and desks.

Then, of course, each room will need a dresser or bureau, and if it doesn't have a closet, an armoire for stashing hang-up clothes. Provide at least six good hangers, not those wire things that come from the dry cleaners. Furnish each guest room with a luggage rack—some innkeepers swear by them as they help keep guests from tossing travel-grimed suitcases on the beds and dressers. And each room should have a full-length mirror. It's extremely frustrating to get all spiffed up for a

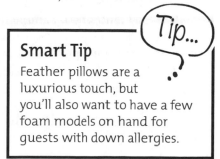

Smart Tip

Feather pillows are a luxurious touch, but you'll also want to have a few foam models on hand for guests with down allergies.

business meeting or night on the town and not be able to check your outfit before you sashay out the door.

The Linen Cupboard

If you're a white sale junkie who can't resist all those linen buys at the department stores, here's your chance to buy big. You'll need lots of linens. Start with two top-quality mattress pads for each bed (economy styles will shred quickly) and two pillows per person—each with its own pillowcase.

Now think about your sheets and your design schemes. Some innkeepers recommend all-white sheets for each and every room. The advantages are that every sheet goes in every room so you don't have to buy as many sets per room and that you can bleach the heck out of any stains with no fear of fading colors or patterns. And pristine white sheets always look crisp, clean and fresh. Other innkeepers like to go with patterned sheets. They can help set the mood of a room, add exciting or romantic color, and give guests the decorating drama they don't give themselves at home.

TV or Not TV

Some B&Bs provide TVs and telephones in each guest room; others choose to provide these features only in common rooms. This is an issue you'll have to work out on your own. If you feel that TVs and phones detract from the old-world ambience of your inn, you may want to leave them out. Most guests, however, will expect to have these items to themselves in their own rooms.

Lots of people can't fall asleep without the stupor induced by the late-night news or Jay Leno; and lots more like to wake up to *Good Morning America* or the *Weather Channel*. And if you plan to cater to business guests, you'll definitely need those in-room phones, along with a desk for the laptop computer.

Another element to consider is that, while some B&Bs, particularly some homestays, provide only common room TVs, not everybody wants to watch the same program at the same time. And a television broadcasting *Survivor* will detract from your Edwardian drawing room's ambience far more than will a set in a private guest room.

Whether you choose white, bold colors or romantic prints, you'll need two to four sets per bed with an equal number of pillow cases. If you'll do your own laundry, you can get away with fewer sets than if you send out your linens and have to wait for them to come back. You'll also need one blanket per bed, with an extra tucked on a handy closet or wardrobe shelf for guests to grab if they get chilly.

> **Tip...**
>
> **Smart Tip**
>
> If your shower won't boast glass doors, go for a fabric curtain backed by a plastic or vinyl one. This looks much more elegant than the drab plastic variety.

The pièce de résistance, of course, is the quilt, comforter or designer bedspread on each bed. You'll need matching dust ruffles and pillow shams and inexpensive pillows to tuck into the shams. Plan on a few extra bedspreads that can be used interchangeably in all rooms to have at the ready for stain emergencies.

Bathing Beauties

Guest bathrooms should be beauties—like the king-sized bed, they're an area in which you can wow guests. As you know from our renovations section, whirlpool tubs are a grand touch. But even if you can't provide them, you can go impressive with matching faucets, handles, and towel bars and cabinet drawer pulls. If you've got brass faucets on the sink, for instance, install brass faucets in the shower or tub, brass towel bars, and brass or other complementary drawer pulls as well.

Towels, besides being a necessity, can also make a statement. As with sheets, you can opt for all-white or you can go eclectic with color and pattern. Either way, you'll want sets comprising at least one bath towel, one face towel, and one wash cloth per person. Plan on two to four sets per person, per stay, plus a few extras for emergencies or bath-fanatic guests, depending on how you'll handle laundry. Some innkeepers change towels every day even when guests stay for a week or more. Others opt to change them every second or third day for longer-staying guests. Don't forget the bath mat—one that can easily go from floor to laundry and back again.

If you'll be beach or poolside, make sure you have more casual towels and that you specify their use. Especially at the beach, guests may wander down to the sand with towels and neglect to bring them back. If you have Wal-Mart specials, it's not so bad, but if they lose part of your set of luxury extra-thick bath towels, you'll be unhappy.

All bathrooms should have excellent lighting, especially over the vanity mirror so guests can see to shave, arrange their hair, and apply makeup. A special lighted makeup mirror with one side magnified is also a nice touch.

Give guests plenty of room to spread out their toiletries. If you'll have pedestal sinks, you might consider a small dresser or table; if you have a counter-type sink, don't put so much bric-a-brac on it that there's no room for guests' things.

You'll also need soaps. You can purchase those hotel-size bars in a variety of sizes at janitorial or hotel suppliers to stock on the sink and in the tub or shower. Or stock liquid soaps with fun fragrances. Just make sure to use plastic containers in the tub and shower for safety. For extra luxury, set out baskets of small-size bubble baths, bath oils, herbal soaps, lotions, shampoos, and conditioners. And don't forget tissues, extra toilet paper, drinking glasses, and a wastebasket. And for the ultimate in luxury, you might stock your own logo-embroidered bath robes.

The Kitchen and Dining Area

How and where you serve guests is entirely up to you. Some B&Bs, particularly small homestays, feed guests in the kitchen breakfast nook right along with family. Others serve elegant meals in the formal dining room; still others deliver breakfasts to the bedrooms. And, of course, many inns serve breakfasts alfresco on the porch or in the garden on fine, sunny mornings. There's no right or wrong—just whatever works best for you and your situation.

Unless you plan to deliver breakfast to your guest rooms, you'll need to consider how many guests you'll serve in the kitchen or dining room at once. You don't want more diners than you have chairs. Some innkeepers with small dining facilities and a large number of guests have cruise-ship style seatings and ask guests to sign up for the times they want to eat. If you serve continental breakfasts, you'll need a sideboard or buffet on which to set out your food.

No matter how you serve, you'll need plenty of dishes, tableware, and serving utensils. And especially if you'll have a historic home, like a Victorian, and want to feature elegant breakfasts or teas, you'll want the sort of dishes that don't come with Corell Livingware or Melmac—things like berry bowls, jelly dishes, dessert stemware, relish trays, and butter bowls. If you'll serve wine or sherry or provide champagne for honeymoons or other romantic evenings, you'll need special stemware. Don't forget glasses for everything from morning orange juice to afternoon lemonade—guests can drink out of plastic Pokémon cups at home. When they vacation with you, they want elegance. Stock plenty of tablecloths or placemats and cloth napkins—one napkin per guest per meal.

You'll want two coffee makers or a model with two brewing centers—one for full-bore caffeine and one for decaf. And you'll want a tea kettle and teapots as well. Tea is becoming an "in" drink to (well, almost) rival coffee, and some guests prefer herbal tea blends over any sort of caffeinated drink. If you'll serve guests in

Smart Tip

Tip...

Keep a supply of top-quality dinner-size paper napkins in the pantry for the rare occasion when you run short of clean cloth ones.

their rooms, you'll need thermal carafes or pots for each room, as well as serving trays or carts.

A refrigerator with an icemaker will make your life far easier. And you should also, in fact, consider an extra refrigerator for guests. Guests frequently want to stash cold drinks, picnic repasts, or the previous evening's restaurant doggie bags in a fridge. Giving them one of their own takes the pressure off yours.

Laundry and Cleaning Center

If you're not currently Mr. or Ms. Clean, you will be as soon as you open your B&B doors. You'll do great loads of laundry on a daily basis, carry toilet brushes as soldiers carry rifles, and become intimate with vacuum cleaners and cleaning supplies of every description. You'll want a utility center that puts all this easily at hand.

Even if you go with a laundry service, you'll need at least one washer and dryer. If you'll do it all yourself, you may want two stackable washer/ dryer units or one heavy-duty washer and two dryers. Give yourself—just like at the laundromat—plenty of room to spread out and fold sheets and towels, and a large linen cupboard or closet in which to store all those extras. Don't forget an ironing board and iron for yourself as well as a loaner or two for guests. You'll also need space to store vacuums, carpet cleaners, brooms, mops, dustpans, and all those cleaning supplies and the caddies to carry them in. Purchase

Smart Tip

If you'll have various sizes of bedding, label shelves so you don't tromp upstairs to make the king bed only to discover you've brought queen sheets.

cleaning products in bulk at janitorial supply stores; their products aren't the ones you see advertised on TV, but they work as well or better, and are far less expensive than the ones on the supermarket shelf or even at a discount supplier like Sam's Club or Costco.

Renovation Checklist

Your renovation may require more or less than the items on this list; be sure to check with a reputable professional. This list will get you started.

Electrical

❑ If only 110 v to house, bring in 220 v

❑ If necessary, change panel and add circuits for:

___ HVAC (heating, ventilation, and air conditioning)

___ Water heater(s) (unless gas water heaters)

___ Washer(s) and dryer(s)

___ Dishwasher

___ Disposal

___ Small kitchen appliances

___ Kitchen range hood

❑ Add receptacles where necessary for bathrooms, bedrooms, and common areas

❑ Add GFIs (ground-fault interrupters) to all kitchen and bath receptacles

❑ Attic fan

❑ Hard-wired smoke detectors

❑ Exterior house lights

❑ Walkway and parking area lights

❑ Garden, sign, and security spotlights

❑ Other exterior electrical such as fountain, hot tub, swimming pool, well pump

❑ GFI to hot tub

❑ Ventilation fans in bathrooms, if no windows

❑ Heat lamp or wall heaters in bathrooms, if no HVAC

Exterior

❑ Walkways level and free of obstructions or tripping hazards

❑ Steps, if painted wood, slip-resistant

❑ Stair rails sturdy and secure

❑ Wheelchair ramp, if necessary and/or desired

Renovation Checklist, continued

❑ Paint

❑ Roof structurally sound and looks attractive

❑ Gutters, soffits, and wood trim structurally sound and attractive

❑ Exterior wood and sidings in good condition

❑ Replace door hardware, if necessary

❑ Adequate parking, resurfaced or striped, if necessary

Interior Finishing Touches

❑ Add crown and base moldings and chair rails, if desired

❑ Wallpaper and/or borders

❑ Window coverings

❑ Full-length mirrors in bedrooms

❑ Ceiling fans

❑ Wall sconces for reading light in guest rooms

❑ Fireplaces and mantels

❑ Paint

❑ Coordinating bathroom faucets, handles, towel bars, and cabinet hardware

❑ Vanity cabinets or pedestal sink with nearby counter space

❑ Tub with shower or whirlpool with shower

❑ Separate shower

❑ Bidet, if desired

❑ Master-keyed guest room doors

Phone and Cable

❑ Install private phone lines to all rooms if using guest phone system

❑ Install cable to all rooms for TV, if desired

❑ Adequate phone lines to handle guest phone system, computer, fax, and electronic credit card

Plumbing

❑ Adequate drainage for washing machine(s)

❑ 2" and 4" drain lines for showers, tubs, and toilets

Renovation Checklist, continued

❑ Hot and cold water lines for new bathrooms

❑ Adequate hot water system: water heater(s)—extra water heater, if necessary

❑ Water-saving toilets, faucets, and shower heads (unless retaining antiques)

❑ Enlarge drain field if on septic, if necessary

❑ Gas lines for fireplaces in guest and common rooms

❑ Add well, if necessary

❑ Sprinkler watering system

Walls and Floors

❑ Insulate all exterior walls for energy conservation

❑ Insulate walls between rooms for soundproofing

❑ Heavy insulation in attic for energy conservation

❑ Add storm windows or double-insulated glass, if possible

❑ 32" or more wheelchair-width doors, if necessary and/or desired

❑ Repair or refinish drywall or plaster

❑ Refinish hardwood floors

❑ Ceramic tile or linoleum

❑ Carpet

Other

_____

_____

Furnishings Checklist

Your furnishings should reflect the character and tone of your B&B. Use this list as a guide—add or improve in any ways that suit your operation and make it truly special.

Common Areas

❑ Front desk or check-in desk and chairs

❑ Writing desk and chair

❑ Sofa

❑ Loveseat

❑ Armchairs and/or side chairs

❑ Coffee table

❑ Side tables

❑ Card table and chairs

❑ Reading lamps

❑ Accent lamps

❑ Hat or coat rack

❑ Umbrella stand

❑ Mirror for foyer

❑ Books and magazines

❑ Playing cards and games

Guest Bathrooms

Two to four sets per person of the following:

❑ Bath towel, face towel, and washcloth

❑ Bath mat

❑ Beach or pool towels

❑ Lighted makeup mirror

❑ Dresser or table for toiletries (if not enough room on vanity)

❑ Hotel-size soaps or liquid soaps

❑ Bubble baths or bath oils

❑ Lotions, shampoos, and conditioners

Furnishings Checklist, continued

- ❏ Box of tissues
- ❏ Extra toilet paper
- ❏ Drinking glasses on tray
- ❏ Wastebasket
- ❏ Luxury bath robes

Guest Rooms

- ❏ Bed
- ❏ Mattress and box spring
- ❏ Nightstands
- ❏ Alarm clocks
- ❏ Reading lamps above bed
- ❏ Armchair or straight chair
- ❏ Sofa or loveseat
- ❏ Ceiling fan/light
- ❏ Other reading or accent lamps
- ❏ Dresser or bureau
- ❏ Wardrobe or armoire
- ❏ Luggage rack
- ❏ Full-length mirror
- ❏ Two to four sets of sheets and pillows per bed
- ❏ Two blankets
- ❏ Quilt, comforter, or bedspread
- ❏ Dust ruffle

Kitchen and Dining

- ❏ Dining table(s) and chairs
- ❏ Sideboard or buffet
- ❏ Cups, dishes, and servingware
- ❏ Stemware and/or glasses
- ❏ Tablecloths or placemats

Furnishings Checklist, continued

❑ One cloth napkin per guest per meal
❑ Two coffee makers
❑ Tea kettle
❑ Teapots
❑ Thermal carafes
❑ Serving cart
❑ Serving trays
❑ Guest refrigerator

Laundry and Cleaning Center

❑ Washer(s) and dryer(s)
❑ Ironing board—one or two extra for guests
❑ Iron—one or two extra for guests
❑ Vacuum cleaner—one per floor
❑ Broom—one per floor
❑ Mop—one per floor
❑ Dustpan—one per floor
❑ Cleaning products in caddy—one per floor

Porches and Verandas

❑ Rockers
❑ Swing or glider
❑ Tables and chairs for dining
❑ Storage for sand, snow, or hiking gear or bicycles

Other

_____

_____

_____

_____

_____

Purchase, Renovation, and Furnishings Costs

Costs	Pieces of Eight	Lightning Bug Bay
Purchase down payment	$0	$75,800
Closing costs	0	11,572
Bathroom	20,000	45,000
Kitchen	0	4,450
Interior paint	50	5,000
Refinish hardwood floors	0	500
Carpet and pad	3,000	0
Washer/dryer	0	2,500
Water heater(s)	0	300
New master-keyed locks for guest room doors	115	160
Insulation and drywall materials	0	4,000
Wiring and outlets	0	2,000
Guest phone or phone system	60	2,740
Ceiling fans	0	1,000
Central air and heating system	0	5,000
Gas fireplaces in guest rooms	0	5,200
Hard-wired smoke detectors	0	720
Exterior painting	0	15,000
Sign	0	150
Parking and landscaping	2,300	3,500
Furnishings, supplies, and amenities	20,000	60,000
Subtotal	**$45,525**	**$244,592**
Add 10% for unexpected expenses	4,552	24,459
Total Costs	**$50,077**	**$269,051**

8

Getting Up with the Bank

Figuring Your Bottom Line

OK, you've determined how much you'll spend on renovations, furnishings, and supplies—all those start-up costs to get your bed and breakfast ready to roll. Now it's time to figure out what your income and expense bottom line will be. This means first figuring out how much you can charge for your guest rooms and what your occupancy rate should be.

In this chapter, we'll explore all that and more: We'll also investigate your operating expenses—the bills you pay every month for things like phones and utilities—and then put everything together to discover what your actual revenues will be. Then we'll catch up with banks and other lenders to see how you can finance your new inn.

Room Ratings

Your room rates will depend on several factors:

- *The amenities you offer*. You can provide whirlpool tubs, fireplaces, king-size beds, or private balconies to common area features like a swimming pool.
- *Your location*. A bed and breakfast tucked off the beaten track where tourists or businesspeople don't often tread won't be able to charge as much as one in a popular tourist and/or business destination. Your location within your own community can make a difference as well. In a seaside town, for instance, a beachfront B&B can command higher rates than one that's a mile, or even two blocks, off the beach. And an inn in the heart of a popular historic district can demand higher rates than one on the highway leading into town.
- *The going rates in your region*. No matter how upscale your amenities or how desirable your location, your rates will have to be in line with other B&Bs and lodgings in your area. If you charge significantly more, you'll lose business, and—perhaps surprisingly—if you charge significantly less, you'll also lose.

The Price Is Right

Most innkeepers determine their rates through comparison with other local lodging establishments. This is good. You'll have to be in line with others. But you don't necessarily have to toe the line.

Depending on your amenities and your target market, there may be a small margin for creativity. If other similar B&Bs or hotels, for instance, are charging $100 per night, you may be able to get away with charging $105, $115, or possibly even $125 per night—if you can convince potential guests that your inn is worth the extra money.

To do this, you'll need savvy advertising and promotions. This is chancy, especially for the newbie, and it may not work—although some innkeepers believe that if you charge more, guests will automatically believe you're worth it.

(People will think there's something wrong with your inn and won't try you out.)

Everybody's Doin' It

So where exactly do you start? Go back to your market research. Take a look at the rates charged by everybody in your town, from budget motels to luxury hotels to, of course, other bed and breakfasts. Then decide where you fit into the lodging hierarchy. If you're a simple homestay, offering, say, a family atmosphere but not a lot of frills for the hospital patient's relatives or the businessperson in midrelocation, you might want to price your rooms comparably with an upper-range motel or similar B&B. If, on the other hand, you've got luxury amenities and an elegant ambience, you might price your rooms to match those of the luxury hotel or upscale bed and breakfast.

Changing of the Rates

Keep in mind that you probably won't charge the same room rates all year, or even all season. Most lodgings, from the humblest motel to the mightiest hotel, vary their prices with the season. This is especially true in very seasonal areas. In beach towns along Florida's Emerald Coast, for instance, room rates can soar to $70 per night higher during June, July, and August than during the dead of winter.

Depending on your area, you may have a high season, a low season, and one or two "shoulder seasons." If you're in a beach town, for instance, your shoulder seasons may be spring and fall, where you can charge higher than winter rates but not as high as summer.

Weekday Cheapskates

Room rates can vary not only with the season but also with the day of the week. Inns and hotels often offer midweek stays at discounted rates during slower seasons. This is smart—if your area is not highly traveled by vacationers at certain times of the year, the guests you do attract will tend to be weekend-getawayers. Which means you can fill those rooms on Friday and Saturday nights and sit twiddling your thumbs—and losing revenues—the rest of the week. A three-night midweek stay for less than the price of a two-night weekend can encourage guests to

A Room with a View

In fine hotels, the honeymoon suite overlooking the park is more expensive than the tiny room at the back that looks out onto the alley. Follow the same guidelines when pricing your rooms. People will cheerfully pay more for a room with a king-sized bed and a private terrace that overlooks the sea than for an identical room with an identical king-sized bed with a view of the street.

And, as many B&B hosts have discovered, guests will pay even more for the same view and the same bed if they come with "fantasy" amenities like fireplaces and whirlpool tubs.

call in sick, come on down, and fill in your week's calendar. "We give weekday discounts of 10 percent," says innkeeper Marilyn Lewis in Fort Worth, Texas.

Another common practice among lodging establishments is to bump up rates during major holidays and events—anything from a blow-out sports event or convention to a mob-scene annual festival—that they know will bring streams of guests into town.

If you'll play this game, you'll need to consider ahead of time what your rates will be and post them on your rate sheet and web site. While guests never mind when offered an unprinted discount, they'll complain loudly (and with good reason) if your rate sheet says your June through August price is $100 per night, but you charge them $125.

You can get yourself into trouble with this strategy. Carefully check out your competitors' rates before you commit yourself. If you decide to charge extra for New Year's Eve and no other hotel or B&B in your area does so, you just might come up empty on one of winter's highlight nights.

Occupancy Rates

Working up your room rates isn't the only step involved in determining your earnings. You'll also have to determine what your occupancy rates should be. Here again your market research will come in handy. Ask local reservation service organizations what the average annual occupancy rate of comparable lodgings is. According to the Professional Association of Innkeepers International, you should estimate your first year's rate then cut it in half.

If most, for example, have a 60 percent occupancy, then you should expect about 30 percent. Providing you follow through on advertising and marketing, and give your guests a memorable B&B experience, you can add another 10 percent onto your annual occupancy the next year, for an expected 40 percent. The following year you should be able to add on another 10 percent and so on, until you reach the area average.

Like everything else in business—and in life—all this is not set in stone. If you'll start out in an area that's positively screaming for extra rooms, you may be able to command much more than 50 percent of everyone else's average from the get-go. If you've devised a niche that your target market simply can't resist and you do extremely targeted marketing, you may also do better than the norm. And if you buy or lease an existing B&B with a strong customer base, you'll skip past this business-building stage.

But for the most part, you'll want to estimate conservatively. It's much better to do more business than you'd planned, both for you and for your banker and/or investors.

Estimating Earnings

For an idea of how to put all these estimates together to come up with your gross earnings, take a look at the "Estimated Annual Room Revenues" for Pieces of Eight and Lightning Bug Bay on pages 137–139. Then use the worksheet on page 140 to estimate your own annual revenues. This may look frighteningly like an IRS income tax form, but it's really very easy. Follow along as we talk you through it:

1. First decide what your room rates will be. Fill in the name of each room or suite (or number if you won't name your rooms). Write in the amenities underneath each room—this will help you decide how much to charge for each. Fill in your peak season and off-season rates for each room. (To keep this simple, we've eliminated midweek discounts and major holiday or event higher rates. You can add these in if you like.)

2. Figure your total occupancy for one night. This is assuming all your rooms are full and is the most you'll be able to make in one night.

   a. Add up your nightly peak season rates from step 1.

   b. Add up your nightly off-season rates from step 1.

     c. Divide your total nightly peak season rate by your number of rooms. This will give you your average room rate during peak season.

     d. Divide your total nightly off-season rate by your number of rooms. This will give you your average room rate during off-season.

3. Fill in the annual occupancy rate for your area.

4. Determine your maximum possible occupancy for a one-year period: Multiply the number of guest rooms you'll have by 365 nights. This will give you the best possible scenario for your B&B—every room filled every single night of the year.

5. Now you can estimate your occupancy rate for your first year in business:

     a. Take 50 percent of your area's annual occupancy rate (step 3). This figure will represent your estimated occupancy rate for the year.

     b. Multiply your estimated occupancy rate (step 5a) by your maximum possible room nights from step 4. This will give you the number of room nights you can expect in your first year.

     c. Divide those room nights by two (or multiply by 50 percent), which will give you six months of peak season nights and six months of off-season nights. (If your seasons will last more or less than six months, you'll have to use a different percentage.) Multiply the number of peak season nights by your peak average room rate (step 2). This will give you your total peak season revenues.

     d. Multiply the number of off-season nights by your off-season average room rate (step 2). This will give you your total off-season revenues.

     e. Add your total peak and off-season revenues together to get the grand total of your projected annual revenues for your first year.

6. Repeat steps 5a through 5e for each succeeding year, except add 10 percent to each previous year's estimated occupancy rate. If your first year's estimate, for instance, is 30 percent, the second year will be 40 percent, and the third year will be 50 percent.

Cost City

OK, now you know how much you can expect to earn. But you're not done with arithmetic yet. You'll have ongoing operating expenses—the things you pay for every month or every year—to offset all those greenbacks. And until you deduct those costs from your income you won't really know what your bottom line will be. Keep in mind that the figures we're giving here for room-based expenses like towels, food, beverages, and housekeeping supplies, are averages for the newbie B&B. As your occupancy rate climbs, so will those expenses.

On Commission

If you'll go with a reservation service, you'll need to add its commissions into your operating expenses. RSOs typically charge 20 percent to 30 percent of each bill for guests they direct to you and deduct their commissions before sending guests' payments to you. This is usually done on a monthly basis.

Call Your Shots

As we explored in our start-up chapter, if you've got a business, you probably need a couple of phone lines. You definitely need a separate business line. Depending on the capabilities of your phone service provider, you should be able to put your fax machine on "distinctive ring." This service is much cheaper than a completely separate phone line for the fax machine and you still get a distinct fax number to hand out. When there is an incoming fax, the phone ring is "distinct" from the regular ring of whatever line you have it attached to. However, if you get a lot of faxes, you won't want this to tie up your business line so think it through carefully (you can always change if it isn't working out, and you can typically still keep your same fax number). You will almost definitely want broadband (cable) internet service, not dial up, so internet use never ties up your phone line—plus dial up is so slow that it has become a term used to mean slow! Then you'll need to add more lines for guest phones. If you'll install a special phone system that sends calls to guests' rooms, you'll want at least two extra lines. If you go with a single, toll-call-restricted phone for guests, you'll need one extra line.

Estimate a base rate of $30 per month for each line; add in another $3 to $5 per month for toll-call restriction service if you're going that route. If you choose the guest phone system, you'll need roll-over service, which permits a busy line to roll, or switch, over to one that's not busy for incoming or outgoing calls. Expect to pay about $20 per line for this feature.

Now add in estimated long-distance charges for your primary business line, based on where your potential guests will be located, how often you expect to call them, and what sort of rate you've negotiated with your long-distance carrier.

You may also want to consider making your business line toll-free to encourage calls from potential guests. Since a toll-free line is not free to you—you pay for incoming calls as if they're placed collect—the costs here will depend on how many calls you receive. If you figure on a base rate of about 12 cents per minute and a year-round average of ten three-minute calls per day, you can add on about $108 per month,

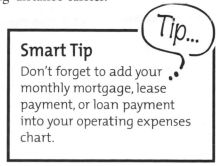

Smart Tip

Don't forget to add your monthly mortgage, lease payment, or loan payment into your operating expenses chart.

or $1,296 per year. Add to that the long-distance carrier's (AT&T, Sprint or whoever) service charge of about $5 per month or $60 a year, for a total of $1,356 annually.

Do you need to have a toll-free number? Absolutely not. It all depends on what your target market is likely to go for and what your nearest competitors are doing. And if you'll start off with an RSO for your first year or two in business, you may want to defer the toll-free issue for at least a few years.

Mail Call

As your business grows, your postage expenses will blossom as well. You'll send out brochures and confirmation letters on a daily basis as well as routine bills, plus the occasional press release and other promotional pieces. For starters, if you assume you'll send at least a few pieces of snail mail per day, you can pencil in about $40 per month for that. If you decide to advertise via direct mail or mail order, your postage costs will be much higher.

The Well-Dressed Office

Once you've dressed your office with stationery and desk accessories, your costs should be fairly low—there's a limit to how many staplers, paper clips, and calendars you'll actually need. Refer to the Office Supplies Mini-Shopping List on page 95 in Chapter 6 for prices.

Getting Webbed

As you know, you'll need some sort of internet service provider as well a web host to give you and your guests access to your web site and e-mail. Plan on $20 to $25 per month if you go with a standard service like AOL, about $50 per month if you choose a cable connection, or $40 to $60 per month if you go with a DSL or ISDN version. Web-hosting fees range from $30 to $50 per month.

Hooked On Utilities

Even if your B&B is the house you've lived in for the last 30 years, your utility bills will be higher than what you pay now. You'll have more people using lights and water. You'll be doing lots of laundry. And you can count on the fact that your guests will keep the heat and air conditioning running at peak levels 24/7, even when it's not that hot or cold outside.

Auto-Matic

You'll want to pencil in a figure for auto expenses. This includes gas for motoring around town to the supermarket, the bakery, and the janitorial supply store, as well as all those trips to the garden center and the home improvement superstore. You'll also want to include routine maintenance costs like oil changes, new tires, and brake jobs.

Keep a log of your auto mileage—the IRS likes this. If you ever get audited, you'll be ready, and you'll know exactly what your mileage is. For purposes of estimating your annual expenses, take a ballpark of your weekly mileage and divide it by your jalopy's miles per gallon. Now multiply that number by whatever gasoline runs per gallon in your area, and then multiply that figure by 52 weeks—like this:

100 mi. per week ÷14 mpg = 7.14 gallons per week

7.14 per week x $2.50 per gallon x 52 weeks = $928.20

Add in a comfortable cushion of $500-$1000 for maintenance, depending on your vehicle's age and propensity for problems, and those are your estimated auto expenses.

Keeping House

You'll need to purchase all those housekeeping and cleaning supplies, plus guest amenities, on a routine basis—everything from those cute little hotel soaps to bubbling baths to lemon-scented bathroom disinfectants. And don't forget about toilet paper and tissues. Your guests won't be pleased if you run out. Allow $400 to $450 per room per year, or $35 to $40 per month.

Throw In the Towels

If you purchase good-quality towels and linens, you shouldn't have much, if any, replacement to worry about immediately. But as time goes by, you'll need to start filling in where

Smart Tip

To avoid those last-minute dashes to the market or janitorial supply house, keep 30 days' worth of housekeeping supplies and guest amenities on hand.

▲

Keeping Up Appearances

Figure in an amount for repairs and maintenance, especially if you'll purchase an old home. Between the age factor of your inn and the added wear-and-tear imposed by even the most well-behaved guests, something is going to need attention—frequently.

A good way to plan for these contingencies is to add in 10 percent of your total income and earmark it "Repairs and Maintenance." Doing so will give you a comfortable cushion for all those mend-it mini-crises that will come up, even in a newer property.

things have gotten stained beyond hope, frayed, or lost. Allow about $125 per room per year, or about $10 per month.

Good Eats

Food and beverages cost money, too. Plan to spend about $75 to $90 per room per month, although these costs can go up or down considerably depending on whether you'll serve a continental breakfast and nothing else, or a hearty lumberjack morning meal, plus wine-and-cheese, cookies, and lemonade, and a late-night hot toddy or chocolate extravaganza.

Helping Hands

Depending on the size of your B&B, your occupancy and energy levels, and your sanity, sooner or later you'll need help. We'll investigate the employee issue in depth in Chapter 10. For now, let's say that as a newbie starting with one part-time assistant, you can figure on $346 per month in your off-season and $700 per month in your high season.

If you'll spring for outsourced services like gardening or pool maintenance, you'll need to add in a figure to cover these costs as well.

Inn the Money

Once you've estimated your operating expenses, you can deduct them from your annual profits to put together an income and expense statement, and find out what your bottom line will be. Look at the income and expense statements of Pieces of

Eight and Lightning Bug Bay B&Bs on pages 141 and 142, then pencil in your own using the worksheet on page 143.

You'll want to tailor your income statement to your particular bed and breakfast; you may or may not need to ink in figures for items like mortgage and employee payroll. But you will need to figure in property taxes, business licenses, membership fees for professional associations, and legal and accounting fees.

Keep in mind that your first years will be your leanest; most bed and breakfasts don't really become profitable until their third, fourth, or even fifth years. For instance, Pieces of Eight's owners will only be able to pocket a tad over $1,600 at the end of their first year. That's based on a low first year occupancy rate of 30 percent, or $29,554. By their fourth year in business, however, they'll have a far higher occupancy rate and should be able to bring in $59,130.

They'll also, of course, have higher utilities and food/beverage expenses, but these should be balanced by the B&B having built enough of a clientele to be able to drop the RSO and its commissions. Which means that by year four, Pieces of Eight's owners can expect to earn net revenues in the neighborhood of $30,000.

Banking On It

Now that you've done the math, you may be ready to roll—or not, depending on the state of your wallet. If you can easily afford the start-up funds, which will include not only the purchase, renovations, and furnishings costs you calculated in Chapter 7 but also the office start-up expenses you figured in Chapter 6, go for it.

If, on the other hand, your coffers won't stand the strain, you'll have to find financing. This is not a terrible thing—you've got all those lovely expenses figures and that projected income statement to show prospective lenders.

You might want to consider financing through your local bank or credit union. Romancing the bank is not an easy task. Like actors and authors, you need to be able to take rejection on the chin and bounce back, then find another bank to woo. You also need to be prepared to fill out endless forms and answer questions that should (seemingly) be no one's business but your own. But it can be done.

The more information you have the happier your banker will be. Put together a package that includes not only your start-up costs statement and projected income and expense statement,

> **Tip...**
>
> **Smart Tip**
> To make the best possible impression on your banker, assemble your start-up materials in a professional-looking folder along with your desktop-published brochure or price lists. The more businesslike your company looks, the better.

but everything else you can think of. Make charts or reports with all those statistics you've gathered in your market research to illustrate that the B&B industry has a sunny future and that the target market and location you've chosen are viable. All of this will be part of something called a business plan.

Friends and Family

If you can't—or don't want to—go with a bank loan, try borrowing from family and/or friends. This source has several advantages: minimal paperwork, no application fees or lengthy waiting period, and the satisfaction of sharing your business success with your lenders.

Whether you borrow from Great Aunt Myrtle or your best friend, Bob, however, keep in mind that it's still a business loan. Figure the repayment of borrowed funds into your costs, and treat your repayment agreement as seriously as you would any bank loan.

Going Plastic

Yet another option for B&B start-up funds is as close as your back pocket—your credit cards. Before you choose this option, take a look at your available credit balances and the annual percentage rates. Card companies frequently offer low, low rates as an incentive to sign up or to use their service. Go with the one that offers the best rate for the longest period. There are other start-up financing avenues besides the ones we've explored here.

Business Plan in Brief

A business plan is not only a key factor in presenting your business to a prospective lender, it is also a key piece of your own planning and future management of your business. You don't have to stick to your plan word-for-word—but without a plan, you are not deviating from anything, you're just winging it.

There are hundreds of books available to help you do a business plan for your bed and breakfast, so we won't spend lots of time on it here. The key point is, do one. Most of the components of the business plan—revenue projections, outline of the business set-up, projected income and expense sheets (see the sample forms on pages 143 and 144)—are all things good business owners are preparing anyway just to get a clear view of the business they are getting into. An "Income and Expense Worksheet" for your B&B is provided on page 145.

Pull all this into a presentable package and use it to present your business to the bank. It proves you are organized and have seen a clear overall picture of your business as a start-up and one to five years from now.

Pieces of Eight B&B Estimated Annual Room Revenues

Room Rates

The Captain's Stateroom:	King bed, private balcony overlooking the sea	$100/night peak season; $50/night off-season
The Smugglers' Chamber:	King bed, private balcony overlooking the sea	$100/night peak season; $50/night off-season
The Secret Chamber:	Queen bed in a tower room	$85/night peak season; $42.50/night off-season
The Pirate's Lady's Chamber:	Queen bed overlooking the garden	$85/night peak season; $42.50/night off-season

Total Occupancy for One Night

$370/night peak season ÷ 4 rooms = $92.50 average room rate

$185/night off-season ÷ 4 rooms = $46.25 average room rate

Annual Area Occupancy Rate: 60%

Number of Guest Rooms: 4

Maximum Occupancy: 4 x 365 nights = 1,460 room nights

Year 1 Occupancy	Income	**Year 2 Occupancy**	Income
50% x 60% = 30% occupancy		10% + 30% = 40% occupancy	
30% x 1,460 = 438 nights		40% x 1,460 = 584 nights	
219 peak room nights x $92.50 =	$20,257	292 peak roinights x $92.50 =	$27,010
219 off-season room nights x $46.25 =	10,128	292 off-season room nights x $46.25 =	13,505
	$30,385		**$40,515**

Year 3 Occupancy	Income	**Year 4 Occupancy**	Income
10% + 40% = 50% occupancy		10% + 50% = 60% occupancy	
50% x 1,460 = 730 nights		60% x 1,460 = 876 nights	
365 peak room nights x $92.50 =	$33,762	438 peak room nights x $92.50 =	$40,515
365 off-season room nights x $46.25 =	16,881	438 off-season room nights x $46.25 =	20,257
	$50,643		**$60,772**

Lightning Bug Bay B&B Estimated Annual Room Revenues

Room Rates

The Eagle's Lair Suite:	King bed, sofa sleeper, whirlpool tub, fireplace, lake/forest view	$150/night peak season; $75/night off-season
The Timber Wolf Suite:	King bed, sofa sleeper, whirlpool tub fireplace, lake/forest view	$150/night peak season; $75/night off-season
The Lake Lodge Room:	King bed, whirlpool tub, fireplace, lake view	$100/night peak-season; $50/night off-season
The Lake View Room:	King bed, whirlpool tub, fireplace, lake view	$100/night peak season; $50/night off-season
The Lake Mist Room:	King bed, whirlpool tub, fireplace, lake view	$100/night peak season; $50/night off-season
The Whispering Pines Room:	Twin beds, fireplace, forest view	$85/night peak season; $42.50/night off-season
The Deerpoint Room:	King bed, fireplace, forest view	$85/night peak season; $42.50/night off-season
The White Birch Room:	King bed, fireplace, forest view	$85/night peak season; $42.50/night off-season

Lightning Bug Bay B&B Estimated Annual Room Revenues, continued

Total Occupancy for One Night

$855/night peak season ÷ 8 rooms = $107 average room rate

$428/night off-season ÷ 8 rooms = $53.44 average room rate

Annual Area Occupancy Rate: 60%

Number of Guest Rooms/Suites: 8

Maximum Occupancy: 8 x 365 nights = 2,920 room nights

Year 1 Occupancy	Income
50% x 60% = 30% occupancy	
30% x 2,920 = 876 nights	
438 peak room nights x $107 =	$46,866
438 off-season room nights x $53.44 =	23,406
	$70,272

Year 2 Occupancy	Income
10% + 30% = 40% occupancy	
40% x 2,920 = 1,168 nights	
584 peak room nights x $107 =	$62,488
584 off-season room nights x $53.44 =	31,208
	$93,696

Year 3 Occupancy	Income
10% + 40% = 50% occupancy	
50% x 2,920 = 1,460 nights	
730 peak room nights x $107 =	$78,110
730 off-season room nights x $53.44 =	39,011
	$117,121

Year 4 Occupancy	Income
10% + 50% = 60% occupancy	
60% x 2,920 = 1,752 nights	
876 peak room nights x $107 =	$93,732
876 off-season room nights x $53.44 =	46,813
	$140,545

Estimated Annual Room Revenues Worksheet

1. Determine your room rates:

Room: _____ $ _____ /night peak season

Amenities: _____ $ _____ /night off-season

Room: _____ $ _____ /night peak season

Amenities: _____ $ _____ /night off-season

Room: _____ $ _____ /night peak season

Amenities: _____ $ _____ /night off-season

Room: _____ $ _____ /night peak season

Amenities: _____ $ _____ /night off-season

Room: _____ $ _____ /night peak season

Amenities: _____ $ _____ /night off-season

Room: _____ $ _____ /night peak season

Amenities: _____ $ _____ /night off-season

Room: _____ $ _____ /night peak season

Amenities: _____ $ _____ /night off-season

Room: _____ $ _____ /night peak season

Amenities: _____ $ _____ /night off-season

Estimated Annual Room Revenues Worksheet, continued

2. **Figure your total occupancy for one night:**

   a. Add together all your $ _____ /night peak seasons from 1 above:

   b. Add together all your $ _____ /night off-seasons from 1 above:

   c. $ _____ /night peak season (2a) ÷ _____ rooms = $ _____ peak season average room rate

   d. $ _____ /night off-season (2b) ÷ _____ rooms = $ _____ off-season average room rate

3. **Note your annual area occupancy rate:** _____ %

4. **Figure your maximum possible annual occupancy:** _____ rooms × 365 nights = _____ room nights

5. **Figure your first-year occupancy:**

   a. Year 1 Occupancy: 50% × _____ area annual occupancy rate = _____ %

   b. _____ % (last percent in 5a) × _____ (your max. room nights from 4 above) = _____ room nights

   c. _____ room nights (from 5b) ÷ 2 = _____ peak room nights × $ _____ (peak average room rate from 2 above) = $ _____

   d. _____ room nights (from 5b) ÷ 2 = _____ off-season nights × $ _____ (off-season average room rate from 2 above) = $ _____

   e. Add _____ (5c) and _____ (5d) = $ _____ your first-year occupancy

6. **Figure your second-year occupancy:**

   a. Year 2 Occupancy: 50% × _____ area annual occupancy rate = _____ % + 10% = _____ %

   b. _____ % (last percent in 6a) × _____ (your max. room nights from 4 above) = _____ room nights

   c. _____ room nights (from 6b) ÷ 2 = _____ peak room nights × $ _____ (peak average room rate from 2 above) = $ _____

   d. _____ room nights (from 6b) ÷ 2 = _____ off-season nights × $ _____ (off-season average room rate from 2 above) = $ _____

   e. Add _____ (6c) and _____ (6d) = $ _____ your second-year occupancy

Estimated Annual Room Revenues Worksheet, continued

7. Figure your third-year occupancy:

a. Year-3 Occupancy: 50% of _____ area annual occupancy rate = _____ % + 10% = _____ %

b. _____ % (last percent in 7a) of _____ (your max. room nights from 4 above) = _____ room nights

c. _____ room nights (from 7b) divided by 2 = _____ peak room nights x $ _____ (peak average room rate from 2 above) = $ _____

d. _____ room nights (from 7b) divided by 2 = _____ off-season nights x $ _____ (off-season average room rate from 2 above) = $ _____

e. Add _____ (7c) and _____ (7d) = $ _____ your third-year occupancy

8. Figure your fourth-year occupancy:

a. Year-4 Occupancy: 50% of _____ area annual occupancy rate = _____ % + 10% = _____ %

b. _____ % (last percent in 8a) of _____ (your max. room nights from 4 above) = _____ room nights

c. _____ room nights (from 8b) divided by 2 = _____ peak room nights x $ _____ (peak average room rate from 2 above) = $ _____

d. _____ room nights (from 8b) divided by 2 = _____ off-season nights x $ _____ (off-season average room rate from 2 above) = $ _____

e. Add _____ (8c) and _____ (8d) = $ _____ your fourth-year occupancy

Pieces of Eight B&B

INCOME & EXPENSE STATEMENT
For the Year Ended December 31, 20xx
(First Year In Operation)

Income

Room revenues	$29,554

Expenses

Mortgage	0
Property tax	2,000
Phone	550
Toll-free line	0
Utilities	1,800
Electronic card processing	0
Miscellaneous postage	360
Licenses	200
Insurance	1,500
Legal services	360
Accounting services	300
Office supplies	120
Professional memberships	175
Auto expenses	600
Advertising	500
Web hosting	360
Internet service	240
RSO commissions	3,900
Housekeeping/amenities	1,600
Towel/linen replacement	100
Food and beverage	3,600
Employees	0
Gardening service	0
Loan repayment	5,724
Repair and maintenance	2,950

Total Expenses	**−26,939**
Net Annual Income or Loss	**$2,615**

Note: Loan repayment based on $50,000 (renovation and furnishings costs) borrowed at 8 percent interest for 15 years.

Lightning Bug Bay B&B

INCOME & EXPENSE STATEMENT
For the Year Ended December 31, 20xx
(First Year In Operation)

Income

Room revenues	$70,272
Phone (Guests' long-distance charges)	50
	$70,322

Expenses

Mortgage	$26,412
Property tax	4,500
Phone	1,200
Toll-free line	1,360
Utilities	3,600
Electronic card processing	420
Miscellaneous postage	500
Licenses	300
Insurance	3,000
Legal services	360
Accounting services	300
Office supplies	170
Professional memberships	300
Auto expenses	900
Advertising	1,000
Web hosting	360
Internet service	240
RSO commissions	9,275
Housekeeping/amenities	3,200
Towel/linen replacement	200
Food and beverage	7,200
Employees	6,276
Gardening service	900
Loan repayment	0
Repair and maintenance	7,000
Total Expenses	**−78,973**
Net Annual Income or Loss	**$-8,651**

Notes: Mortgage based on $379,000 purchase price, 20% down. $300,000 mortgage loan at 8 percent interest for 30 years. Owners used the proceeds from the sale of their previous home to finance their down payment and closing costs as well as their renovation and furnishing costs.

Income and Expense Statement Worksheet

Income

Room revenues $ _____

Expenses

Mortgage   _____

Property tax   _____

Phone   _____

Toll-free line   _____

Utilities   _____

Electronic card processing   _____

Miscellaneous postage   _____

Licenses   _____

Insurance   _____

Legal services   _____

Accounting services   _____

Office supplies   _____

Professional memberships   _____

Auto expenses   _____

Advertising   _____

Web hosting   _____

Internet service   _____

RSO commissions   _____

Housekeeping/amenities   _____

Towel/linen replacement   _____

Food and beverage   _____

Employees   _____

Gardening service   _____

Loan repayment   _____

Repair and maintenance   _____

Total Expenses $ _____

Net Annual Income or Loss $ _____

9

Breakfast in Bed
Daily Operations

Ok, you've worked your way through all the renovations, sweated out the finances, and are still reading. Good—you've got drive and perseverance, two stellar qualities for the B&B innkeeper. Now, at last, it's time to start hosting.

In this chapter, we'll explore the daily life of the bed-and-breakfast host. We'll take reservations, greet guests, serve those scrumptious breakfasts, handle housekeeping, and investigate the ins and outs of dealing with people.

Reservations Please

Unless you rely on a reservation service for all your bookings, you'll spend a fair amount of time fielding inquiries from prospective guests and making reservations. It's fun and rewarding (after all, every booked night on your calendar is another dollar for you), but it's also important that you handle it properly. Aside from your web site or guidebook entry, your voice on the phone will be guests' first impression of your B&B. The manner in which you treat them and the answers you give to their questions will make a lasting impression.

Spin City

Always answer the phone in a cheerful, confident manner. Even if the roof's leaking from some mysterious, untraceable source, the dishwasher's spewing suds all over the kitchen floor, the neighbor's dog dug up and ate the 200 daffodil bulbs you planted yesterday, and your kids just got sent home from school with the stomach flu, you need to sound as if all is right with the world.

Some prospective guests are "window shopping," deciding between you and several other B&Bs. Others have basically already made up their minds to stay with you and just want confirmation that you're the right choice. Either way, your salesmanship may make the difference between making a reservation and a pass.

This can mean walking a bit of a fine line. While you want to paint the brightest possible picture of your inn and your surroundings, it doesn't pay to tamper with the truth. If your view of the lake consists of a glimmer of blue through the trees, for instance, and a caller asks about the view or your proximity to the lake, don't lie. Your guest will be disappointed when she arrives, and things will go downhill from there. Instead, say something like "We're not right on the lake, so you won't have a panoramic view. We do get glimpses of that gorgeous blue among the trees and wonderful cool breezes off the lake all summer. And the beach is only a five-minute walk through the pines."

This way you're being truthful; nobody's going to be disappointed. But you're also putting a spin on things, giving your caller other positives to ponder instead of a flat negative.

Make a Date

Discussing arrival and departure dates can get confusing. Guests will give you the date they're leaving home instead of the date they're arriving, which may be one day later. They'll say they want to check out on Saturday when they mean they want to spend Saturday night and leave Sunday. They'll look at the wrong calendar page and give you May's dates when they mean June's.

And having guests arrive when you don't expect them—or when you don't even have a place to put them—isn't fun. So make sure you clarify everything as carefully as possible. Don't make a reservation if you don't have your reservations calendar in front of you, either on your computer screen, on your desk, or in your hand. And always, always write everything down or fill it in on your computer screen while you have the guest on the phone. If you wait until later, you'll get sidetracked and run the fearsome risk of not remembering the details. So get in the habit of completing booking information on the spot.

If you'll have only a few guest rooms, you can manage fairly well with a hand-drawn calendar, but if you'll have four or more, you'll do much better with a software-created version. Take a look at the "Reservations Calendar" on page 167 and check out the demos offered by various software companies, then make your own decision.

When a guest calls to make a reservation, repeat all the arrival and departure information back to him. Use wording like "OK, I have you arriving Saturday, September 1 and departing Sunday, September 9." Statements like "September 1 to September 9" can be extremely confusing. Some people interpret this as meaning through the 8th while others think it means through the 9th. So be careful!

If your guest comes back with something like "Oh, I thought Sunday was the 12th," or "We wanted to leave on Monday," then you can make changes immediately instead of after your guests are already ensconced in the room, and you've got someone else booked for that same Sunday.

Delineating Deposits

Be sure to clearly state the room rates and your deposit policy. This prevents confusion further down the line, along with unpleasant shocks for both you and your guests. Say something like "That's eight nights at $800. We'll need $200 of that to hold the room for you, which is refundable with at least 10 days' notice. Would you like to put it on a credit card?"

If your caller doesn't want to use her credit card (or you don't take credit cards), let her know that paying by check is fine but that you'll need to receive the deposit within a week.

Deposit policies vary among innkeepers. Some require one night's room rate as a deposit; some ask for 50 percent of the full stay; still others require a flat fee like $100 or $200, regardless of the room rate or the length of stay. The point of the whole thing is to get your guest to commit so you don't lose revenues by holding a room for a guest who fails to show up. Most people, once they've paid the deposit, won't change their minds. If they do, they'll at least give you enough notice to be able to rebook someone else because they don't want to forfeit their deposit.

Along with the amount of deposit you require, you can also choose the length of time for which you'll give refunds. Most B&B hosts require at least one to two weeks notice prior to the check-in date; others willingly settle for 24 hours. Some hosts also retain $5 to $10 of the deposit from a cancelled reservation as a handling fee. In some rare cases, such as during

Smart Tip

Owners of unhosted B&Bs like vacation cottages or condos often require a security deposit—not as a part of the total room fee, but in addition to it. Provided there are no damages or losses, the deposit is refunded after the guests' stay is over.

major holidays or events, you may go with a nonrefundable deposit. Whichever you go with, you must tell your guests when they make the reservations, not several weeks or even months down the line.

You might also introduce some variables into your cancellation policy, such as refunding the deposit if you rebook the room. Or instead of a refund, offering to change the reservation to a different date or to transform the reservation into a gift certificate for the guest to give as a gift to someone else (or herself).

Whichever policy you decide on, keep it consistent. It's unfair to guests (and another legal gray area) to switch back and forth. And it's hard on you, too, having to remember to whom you told what. The fewer variables, the easier your booking life will be.

Party of Five

Ask how many people the guest will be bringing. You don't want to discover after Mr. and Mrs. Smith arrive to check in to that cozy room for two that they've also brought three kids who, they say, "can just plop down on the floor." Most guests, of course, won't consider such a thing, but there will always be a few who'll surprise you.

Which brings us to another place where you'll have to set some policies. Will you mind if guests bring children? This is one of the bigger issues in the innkeeper's world. Since most B&Bs are, by nature, elegant, and romantic establishments, many hosts feel their guests won't want children underfoot; they also worry about fine furnishings suffering at sticky-fingered hands and childproofing everything. These hosts actively discourage children. Other hosts encourage kids. They find them charming guests who delight everyone.

You'll have to decide for yourself where you stand on the youngster front. If you opt for no children, you'll then have to decide how to phrase your policy. No parent wants to hear that you don't want his or her offspring. This is also a sort of legal gray area in some states and downright illegal in others (you are, after all, discriminating against tots), so you'll have to be diplomatic. One way to handle it is to say something like "We find that young children (or kids under 16 or whatever age) don't enjoy themselves at our inn. We can recommend an excellent B&B in town that caters to kids."

Another more friendly and less "gray" way is to devote a separate cottage or carriage house for families, or perhaps a separate wing in your house—if, of course, you have the room to do

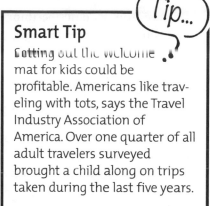

Smart Tip

Setting out the welcome mat for kids could be profitable. Americans like traveling with tots, says the Travel Industry Association of America. Over one quarter of all adult travelers surveyed brought a child along on trips taken during the last five years.

so. Or, just welcome kids and be done with it. You might just find that you'll enjoy them as much as their parents do. (Or more! After all, you'll only have them for a brief visit; then they go home.)

Now, once you're set on the kid factor, and assuming you'll warmly welcome them, you still have to set some ground rules about how many people you allow in a room. Some innkeepers cheerfully provide rollaway beds or cots gratis, some charge $20 or $25 for bringing in a rollaway or cot, and some require that families book a suite, cottage, or carriage house that sleeps more than two. You can set up a suite to sleep from two to six—depending on the room size—by furnishing it with a king or queen bed, a double or queen sofa sleeper, and another queen bed, a loveseat sleeper, or a daybed with a trundle. Some B&B hosts tack on extra fees to the room rate when a suite is occupied by more than two or four people.

The "Bed" in Bed and Breakfast

Which brings us to yet another point to discuss with guests while making reservations: beds. Even if the reservation will be for a couple or a single guest, you'll want to find out their choice in beds—they'll probably ask you anyway. If you can offer a choice of king, queen, or twin, ask which they prefer. If you don't have a choice, say something like "OK, we'll put you in the Snow Queen room, which is one of our most popular. It has a terrific view of Snow Mountain, a king bed, and a private bath with a whirlpool tub." Or "We'll give you the Mountain Hideaway room, which has a double bed and a shared bath."

Note that we've described the other amenities so your guest knows exactly what she's getting. It's fun to let guests discover a few—nice—surprises on arrival, like the window seat tucked into a sunny alcove or the tiny staircase to the widow's walk. But don't leave the usual things, like views, beds and baths, to be discovered—or dismayed by—after check-in.

Be sure, too, to describe things guests may not have considered, like any special parking situations or restrictions, complicated directions (although you're best asking guests to call just prior to leaving home to get these), your smoking or nonsmoking policy, and your pets, if you have them.

Pet Parade

If you're a dog or cat owner as well as an innkeeper, you can't imagine giving up Fido or Fluffy any more than you'd give up one of your kids. But not all your guests will feel the same way. Some people are terrified of even the most docile dog, and many people are allergic to cats and pooches. Still other guests love the homey touch of having a pet on the premises, especially if they're missing their own or can't have one in their apartment.

So what do you do? This is another decision you'll have to make for yourself. The best way to have your dog biscuit and eat it too is to inform prospective guests that your B&B features a resident feline or canine, but that the animal isn't allowed in guest rooms. If this is a problem, you can refer guests to a pet-free inn nearby.

And, of course, it goes without saying that your pets must be as gracious and charming as you are. If there's the slightest chance your dog could decide to nip a guest in the tush (or anywhere else), your cat is prone to scratching people as well as posts, or your poodle likes to doodle on the carpet, forget it.

What about guests who want to bring their own pets along? Industry experts by and large feel that this is a bad idea. Other people's pooches may not be as well-behaved as yours. They may bite, scratch or pee on your furniture, your carpets or your other guests. This could make you liable (for the biting or scratching). And if those pets bring a contingent of fleas along for the ride, you may have an extremely difficult time ridding your house of them long after that guest pet has gone home.

Some determinedly "pet friendly" hosts offer to put up pets as long as their owners keep them in carriers in their own rooms. This doesn't seem very friendly. You might try housing pet guests and their owners in a separate cottage or carriage house and require that pets be kept on leashes at all times.

Check It Out

Once you've established all the other elements of the room reservation, you'll want to make a note of your guest's name, address, and phone number; then make sure she understands your check-in and check-out policy. Say something like "Our check-in time is 2 P.M. to 7 P.M. Check-out is 11 A.M."

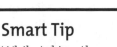

Smart Tip

While taking the reservation, ask guests about any particular food preferences, like vegetarian or vegan, or animal or food allergies.

Most guests will take this at face value and agree. Some, however, will want to know if they can check in earlier or later. This is up to you. Most innkeepers frown on earlier check-ins—they just don't allow enough time to get the rooms cleaned and ready to go for the next batch of guests. On the other hand, it's hard to turn down eager guests standing on your doorstep.

In a perfect world, all guests would arrive only between the hours of 2 and 3 in the afternoon (or whatever's perfect for you). But they don't. Some drive all night from home and show up in your driveway at 9 A.M. Others don't leave home until after work, stop for dinner, get lost, call half a dozen times, and don't appear until midnight.

If you're a full-bore B&B with a staff on-site 24/7, this isn't so bad. When guests arrive, they check in. But if you're a small or homestay operation, you can't sit around all day or night and wait for guests. You've got errands to run, people to see—you've got a life.

While making reservations, ask guests when they expect to arrive so you can plan to be available. Advise them to call you if they run late. You'll forward your business line to your cell phone and, if you're at the market or wherever, you can dash back and meet them. Another alternative is to stash a key for guests under a planter or doormat (or some other creative spot) so they can let themselves in.

For guests who'll arrive really late—after you're normally in bed—you can leave a key and officially check them in the morning. Or wait up until 3 A.M. Or insist that they arrive during your regular business hours.

Whatever method you choose is up to you. Just make sure your guests understand the arrangement and what's expected of them.

Make a Note

Before you disconnect, find out from your guest where she learned about your B&B. This is valuable information that will help in your advertising and marketing efforts. Make a note of this on your reservations form for later use.

Also make a note of special events or tidbits your guest mentions. You don't need to pry. Don't ask "So what will bring you to town?" Most people will freely tell you: It's their honeymoon or anniversary, their daughter's wedding, their nephew's graduation, or the birth of a grandchild. Be sure to mark these events—your guests will be impressed when you greet them on arrival with congratulations or inquiries about the big event. And even more so if you put some commemorative goodie in their room like a tray of heart-shaped chocolates or baby-block cookies.

Use the "Reservation Information" form on page 164 to start yourself off making reservations in style. Modify this form in any way that suits your B&B and your personality. Some innkeepers use a similar form for each guest and file them in manila folders or in a three-ring binder. Others use 4 by 6 cards instead of pages. And others, of course, use computer software (the best alternative unless you're a very small operation). Whatever system you use, make sure you—and whoever else may take reservations—can access it easily.

You're Confirmed

Once you've received your guest's deposit, you can send out a reservation confirmation letter—either by snail mail or e-mail. This is a nice touch that lets guests know their deposit hasn't fallen between the cracks of the U.S. Postal Service or been snatched up by a flaky host who'll never be seen or heard from again.

The confirmation letter adds to the B&B experience. People who are slogging away at that 9-to-5 job all winter can post your confirmation letter on the fridge as a reminder of the summer fun to come. And it gives you a forum in which to spell out your policies and provide—if necessary—written directions and a map to your location.

Cheat Sheet

With everything else you've got going on, it's easy to get sidetracked, flustered, or just plain forgetful when guests call to book rooms. Eliminate goofs by preparing a policy manual or fudge sheet to keep at your reservation desk. This should include:

- ○ Current rate sheet that includes a description of each room (e.g., king-size bed, private bath with whirlpool tub, fireplace, upstairs overlooking the lake)
- ○ Your deposit requirements and cancellation policy
- ○ Your check-in and check-out times
- ○ Your policy on pets and smoking
- ○ Tax cheat sheet that shows room rates including tax

Armed with this cheat sheet and your trusty software or hard copy guest reservation form, you'll be prepared with the proper information at the ring of a phone.

Take a look at the "Reservation Confirmation Letter" on page 165. Then make up your own with any modifications you like.

Welcome Wagon

After all your hard work, the big day finally arrives—your first guests are at the door. And butterflies start dive-bombing your innards. Take a deep breath and relax. You've worked diligently to provide a warm and welcoming atmosphere for your guests, and it will show. They'll enjoy your B&B and you. But just like giving a dinner party, things seem to go more smoothly if you act calm and confident. A flustered, nervous innkeeper makes for uncomfortable guests (not to mention an uncomfortable host).

The first thing to do is answer the door. Because unless you're a larger, well-signed B&B with expected walk-in traffic and a reception desk, guests will knock before entering. (In fact, most bed-and-breakfast hosts keep the front door locked as a matter of course.)

Greet your guests as you would friends who've come for a visit. You can ask about their trip and if they had any trouble with your directions. If you know from your reservation notes that they've come for some special occasion, you can congratulate them on their wedding or anniversary or new grandchild or whatever.

Honey, I Overbooked the Room

Mainstream hotels typically overbook rooms as policy rather than as accident—they figure a certain percentage of guests will fail to show, so overbooking increases the chances of full occupancy. For the B&B building a reputation on personal service, this is not a good policy. But no matter how diligent you are, sooner or later you'll accidentally overbook. It's a hazard of the industry.

The best course of action when this happens is to be honest. Explain the problem, apologize, and then find your guests another place to stay. This is where networking comes in handy. Call other inns, whose hosts you know, and line your guests up with a room. (In return, these hosts will send you their overflow.) If there are no other B&Bs in your area, find guests a room at a hotel or motel.

In a pinch, hosts have been known to offer guests their own bedrooms, pay for the difference if the alternate accommodation is more expensive, or offer a gift certificate for their own B&B at a later date.

We've already explored check-in scenarios, focusing on how to handle guests who'll arrive when you're not home. What if you're on-site, but your guests are early and their room still needs to be cleaned, or the previous guests haven't even checked out yet?

Don't get flustered! Explain the situation and invite your new guests to wait out on the veranda and enjoy the view. Or make themselves comfortable in the parlor and read a vintage magazine. Or take themselves out for some lunch at that cute little place around the corner and come back at check-in time. And don't feel badly about making them wait—even the Ritz has set check-in times and no qualms about sticking to them.

Fun Fact

Americans are great weekend travelers, says the Travel Industry Association of America, and becoming more so all the time. In the last ten-year period surveyed, the number of weekend trips we took rose by 70 percent.

The Grand Tour

Take your guests around your B&B. You'll naturally want to show it off—which is OK because they'll want the grand tour. Point out any special amenities, give them a bit of house history if they ask, and also point out—if it applies in your case and can be seen from the house—the boardwalk to the beach, the path to the lake, or ski slopes, or the bus stop for the downtown route.

While you're at it, you can acquaint guests with your house rules. You don't need to sound like a camp counselor or prison warden, merely a considerate host who's

House Rules

Make up a set of house rules that spells out the same dos and don'ts you give guests during your grand tour, and post one in each room or suite. Rules should be plain and simple but also polite and as friendly as possible. As with your house tour, you want guests to feel welcome and comfortable and not as if they've stumbled into a summer camp barracks or college dorm.

You can go for the hotel-room look and hang your rules on the back of the door, go classier by putting them in an attractive easel-back frame set on a dresser or table, or you can place them on a tray in the room along with, perhaps, a fresh flower, cookie, or chocolate. For an idea of how to word your house rules, take a look at the sample on page 166.

thought out every detail. For instance, instead of saying "Don't smoke. It's not allowed," you can say something like "You know about our in-house nonsmoking policy. If you'd like to smoke, you're welcome to sit out on the deck and enjoy the view."

Show guests how to operate special furnishings or equipment like gas fireplaces or whirlpool tubs. (Many people don't realize, for instance, that you have to fill the tub so the water level is above the jets before turning them on. If not, instant fountain—all over the floor!)

Explain your breakfast policy—whether you serve between, say, 7 A.M. and 10 A.M., have assigned seatings, or will serve them in their rooms. Invite them to participate in afternoon or evening rituals like iced tea on the porch, sherries in the parlor, or sunset on the veranda.

Payment Politics

Next comes the issue of when to ask guests for payment. Novice hosts often feel awkward about asking for money. It seems crass in the midst of your charming welcome patter to suddenly say "OK, now pay me." Some innkeepers prefer to request payment at the end of a guest's stay. Others feel it's best to get it over and done with at the outset.

The upsides to requesting payment at check-in are multifold:

- You don't have to worry that guests will sneak off without paying you.
- If there's any confusion about rates you can clear it up immediately. There's no worry that a guest who spent seven nights in your most expensive suite will

---

Time to Go

Most guests are good about departing promptly at check-out time. Once in a while, however, you'll get the guest who's either chronically tardy and was probably late for her own wedding, or the guest who just doesn't realize when check-out time is.

The best way to handle such a situation is to knock on the door with a pleasant reminder. "Check-out time is 10 A.M. It's now 10:30, and I have another guest booked for your room this afternoon."

For most people, this is all that's necessary. For the rare guest who's dallying because her plane doesn't leave for another three hours, you can offer to keep her bags in the foyer or entry closet while she strolls local shops, or suggest that she sit on the veranda and enjoy the view.

suddenly decided at check-out that he understood he was paying the discount twin-bed room price.

- Guests who need to depart at 5 A.M. to catch that early-morning flight can do so without disturbing you. They just leave their key in the room and they're off.

The downsides of requesting payment upfront are:

- Yes, until you get used to it, it can feel a bit awkward to ask for payment. But that's what you're in business for; your guests understand that. The Ritz and the Waldorf Astoria (or even Motel 6) don't hand over room keys without getting some sort of payment nailed down.

- If your guest decides to stay an extra night or two, you'll have to go through the whole payment process all over again.

- If you'll offer any extras that guests may take advantage of during their stays and that you'll bill for—from long-distance calls to extra wood for the fireplace to a catered candlelit supper for two—then you'll have to take payment at check-out instead of check-in. Otherwise you won't know what those charges might be. The method you choose is up to you. Just make sure you're consistent. If you process one guest at check-in and the next at check-out, sooner or later you'll get confused and either not take a payment at all or ask the same guest to pay up twice, both of which are unpleasant scenarios.

Heavenly Hosting

One of the best parts of innkeeping is meeting new people and making new friends. B&B guests tend to be well-traveled, well-rounded people from all over the world—people you'd like to interact with on a social basis even if you weren't a host. So it's tempting to spend a morning, afternoon, or evening chatting away.

Temper that temptation. Yes, a major factor in the B&B experience for guests is socializing with hosts. But guests don't want to have all their precious vacation time monopolized by you. You must walk another fine line. To be a heavenly host, you should be warm, friendly, and available when guests want to chat. But like a top-drawer butler or parlor maid, you should also be able to withdraw into the woodwork when necessary.

How do you do both at the same time? It's not difficult. Be sensitive to guests' signals.

Bright Idea

If your health department forbids home cooking in your kitchen, or if you don't have the time to prepare luscious baked goods, try buying selections of breakfast goodies from a local bakery to set out on serving platters.

Think about how you'd feel in a similar situation. Say, for instance, you're watering the begonias on the porch and your guests step out, dressed for the beach and toting floats, picnic baskets, and swim fins. Seeing you, they stop and ask how you got started as an innkeeper (something people always want to know). Give them the humorous two-minute version. Then stop. If they sit down and ask for more, you can expand. If they start walking toward the beach, let them go. Don't hold them captive with your entire life story.

Then, of course, there are the guests who want to hear your life story—just when you're madly scrambling to get breakfast on the table or all your rooms cleaned in half an hour. And they never seem to notice you're swamped. To these people, say something along the lines of, "I love to tell that story, but I've got to get ready for my next check-ins. If you're interested, I'd be delighted to share it with you later in the day." Then smile and keep moving. If you stop and wait for approval, you'll be trapped.

Some hosts use shared breakfasts, tea-times, or wine get-togethers as the time to socialize with guests. This is great, so long as you remember the same rules. Don't hold guests captive if they're ready to move on. And like a good party host, allow guests time to meet and mingle with each other as well as with you.

Feeding the Multitudes

This brings us to breakfasts. As you know, you can handle breakfasts in a variety of ways, depending on the rules and regulations of your local health authority, your own quirks and whims, and those of your target market. You can go with any of the following, or devise your own variation:

- *Continental breakfast.* In Europe, this means a roll or croissant, coffee, and sometimes juice. In America, a continental breakfast is typically anything served cold and often prepackaged, including sweet rolls, bagels, individually packaged cold cereals, juice, and coffee or tea. While it's not the most gourmet meal in the world, the continental breakfast has two advantages— you can set it out early and, except for occasional monitoring of hot and cold items, not worry about it, and guests can serve themselves.

- *Real home cooking.* The permutation most people have in mind when they think bed and breakfast, this puts you in the chef's apron turning out scrumptious breakfast breads, delicious egg dishes, and fragrant fruit sides.

> **Tip...**
>
> **Smart Tip**
> Children often don't appreciate gourmet cooking. If your B&B welcomes kids, stock an assortment of kid-targeted cereals, Pop Tarts, and, of course, good old PB&J for picky-eater emergencies.

Gourmet Cheffing

Develop a varied repertoire of recipes for your gourmet breakfasts. Even if your specialty of the house is one that everybody raves about, you'll go bonkers if you have to cook it (and then eat it yourself) over and over and over again. Devise variations on a theme. Instead of your famous blueberry muffins, for instance, use the same recipe but fold in pecans and strawberries, or almonds and chocolate chips.

Experiment with new recipes. But unless you're fairly certain of the results, do those experiments on guest-less days when only your family will (hopefully) have to eat less-than-stellar results.

If things do go awry when you cook for guests, don't panic. Don't apologize. Even famous restaurant chefs goof—more often than you'd guess—and they know that the secret is to improvise. If your gorgeous blueberry breakfast bread collapses into crumbles coming out of the pan, serve it in a bowl with cream and call it Blueberry Morning Crumble. Your guests will never know the difference!

- *Breakfast in a cupboard.* Owners of unhosted B&Bs often shop for breakfast staples like eggs, milk, bread, cereals, and coffee, then store them in cupboards and fridges, ready for guests to prepare their own meals.
- *Breakfast in a basket.* For the unhosted B&B, some hosts deliver—or arrange to have delivered—a selection of muffins and other goodies from a local bakery each morning.
- *Ready breakfast.* Homestay hosts with just one guest or one party of guests prepare a breakfast casserole before leaving for work, then leave it in the oven on warm or in the fridge ready to be popped into the oven.

Time Zoning

As we touched on earlier in this chapter, it's not enough to decide what sort of breakfast you'll offer. You'll also have to decide when and where to serve it. If you go with a continental breakfast, you can serve all morning if you choose. So long as you pop in and out to make sure hot coffees and teas are hot, milk and juices are cold, and that nothing's run dry, all you have to do is whisk away used dishes and crumbs.

Smart Tip

Tip...

Use only distilled water for brewing coffees and teas. It keeps your coffee maker free of hard-water deposits and thus running smoothly for years, but even more important, makes for a far better-tasting cup of java than tap water.

Bright Idea

Set aside pages in your B&B "scrapbook" for guests to write in reviews or comments about restaurants and attractions they've sampled.

But if you'll go with a full breakfast, you'll have to decide how many times a morning you want to cook and serve it. Depending on your energy level, the number of guests in the house, and the amount of seating available, you may want to serve just once, do two seatings, or turn out omelets or pancakes as guests stagger into your kitchen, groping for coffee.

If you'll cater to fishermen who like to be out before dawn, you may need to be up and serving before sunrise. Or set out fixings, and let them serve themselves. If you'll target businesspeople, plan on serving breakfasts at 7 A.M. so they can arrive bright-eyed and bushy-tailed for all those 8 A.M. office conferences.

Walking Guidebook

Your guests will expect you to be a walking guidebook on all facets of your area. They'll ask for advice on local attractions and restaurants, for directions to these sites as well as to the drugstore, mall, gym, and car wash, for referrals to babysitters and chiropractors, for weather forecasts and driving tips.

You should bone up on as much of this as possible, and keep up to date on local special events, new restaurants, and new exhibits or other offerings at local attractions. When guests ask about something to which you don't know the answer, tell them you'll find out, then do so.

Moonlight Serenade

Offer guests romantic candlelit suppers or a serenading violinist without doing any cooking or playing yourself. How? Arrange to have a local caterer or musician take on your guests. The caterer or violinist provides you with his prices, you tack on a "handling fee" to that price, and quote the total amount to your guests.

Your guests are enchanted, the caterer and the musician are happy, and you've got an additional small revenue source—and another niche to set you apart from the crowd.

Put together a three-ring binder or "scrapbook" packed with as much of this information as you can gather. It will save you from answering a lot of questions when you're trying to be four other places at the same time. And guests enjoy paging through your book, planning their day, and daydreaming about their next trip (when, hopefully, they'll stay with you again).

For ideas of what to include in your book, try the following:

- Restaurant menus
- Brochures from local attractions
- Fliers on special events
- Maps and directions to shops, gas stations, the mall, the gym, the drugstore
- Maps and directions to local attractions, events, and historic districts
- Phone numbers of general practitioners, pediatricians, chiropractors
- Phone number of your real estate agent (guests often like to look at property and dream of buying a vacation getaway or starting their own B&B)
- Seasonal weather tips
- Area warnings like the meanings of surf or ski condition flags, hiking trail guidelines, or big-city safety tips
- Cable TV channel key (e.g., Channel 7 is the Weather Channel, Channel 8 is HBO)

King or Queen of Clean

As an innkeeper, you'll spend a great deal of time as a hotel maid—the king or queen of clean. Just how much time you'll devote will depend on the number of rooms, the number of guests you have at any one time, and whether you have help or do it all yourself. Naturally, a homestay with two guest rooms will present far fewer demands than a B&B with six rooms.

You'll soon get into a routine that will have you flying from one room to the next. There really isn't that much to do—one guest room is a lot less work than cleaning the whole house. As a rule of thumb, expect to spend about a half-hour on each room and its private bath, sailing through the following:

> **Bright Idea**
> Keep a wet/dry vacuum in your cleaning cupboard arsenal. It will come in handy for cleaning sundry spills and mopping up after plumbing crises.

- Strip beds. If time allows, pop linens in washer and then dryer. If not, take a fresh set from linen storage.

- Strip towels and bath mat from bathroom. If time allows, pop towels in washer and then dryer. If not, take a fresh set from linen storage.
- Empty wastebaskets.
- Scour toilet, tub, shower, and sink.
- Mop bathroom floor.
- Vacuum guest room.
- Dust guest room.
- Clean mirrors in guest room and bathroom.
- Discard faded fresh flowers or greenery and replace with fresh if applicable.
- Make beds.
- Stock bathroom with fresh or freshly laundered towels and bath mat.
- Replace soaps and bubble baths or other amenities.

And that's about it. You can touch up guest rooms and baths when you replace linens and towels. During your off-season, you'll do (or hire someone to do) your "deep cleans," the spring cleaning stuff like scrubbing baseboards, waxing floors, oiling furniture, and shampooing carpets.

Sharing the Load

Shared bathrooms require a bit more work. Even though you'll provide guests with towel racks in their rooms, they may leave towels draped over the shower rod and washcloths festooned on the sink. And even though you ask that they keep the bathroom clean for the next guest, chances are they won't scrub out that sink or tub.

Make it a habit to check the shared bath each time you pass by. Replace towels and washcloths. Rinse the sink, scour the tub, and give the toilet a sudsing. Empty the wastebasket and restock soaps and amenities. It won't take long and it will keep the bath tidy and fresh for each new guest.

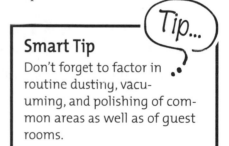

Smart Tip
Don't forget to factor in routine dusting, vacuuming, and polishing of common areas as well as of guest rooms.

Reservation Information

1. Guest name _____

2. Guest address _____

3. Guest business phone _____

4. Guest home phone _____

5. Guest e-mail address _____

6. Dates and days reserved _____
   (e.g., arriving Sunday June 1, and departing Wednesday, June 4)

7. Room reserved _____

8. Number of guests in party _____

9. Room rate/night _____

10. Room price for total stay _____

11. Deposit _____

12. Deposit due date _____

13. Payment method _____
    _____
    (If credit card, record card type [Visa, MasterCard or American Express], card number, expiration date, and cardholder name)

14. How did guest learn of your B&B? _____

15. Food preference or allergies _____
    _____

16. Guest notes _____
    (e.g., guests coming for special occasion like honeymoon or anniversary, to visit new grandchild, or whatever)

17. Deposit paid on what date _____ Amount paid _____

18. Balance due on price of total stay _____

19. Confirmation letter sent by mail or e-mail on what date _____

20. Rollaway or cot needed _____

Reservation Confirmation Letter

Gull Cottage
Bed & Breakfast

A Seaside Cottage Out of Time

January 8, 20xx

Ms. Angelica Arnaud
600 Morning Glory Lane
Midvale, MI 46000

Hi, Angelica!

Thank you for your deposit on the Sea Siren Room at Gull Cottage. We have reserved your dates. We show you arriving Sunday, April 1, 20xx, and departing Saturday, April 7.

Your rental rate, due on check-in, is $663.00. This includes all taxes. The Sea Siren Room has a king-sized bed, private bath with a whirlpool tub, and a fireplace.

Gull Cottage is a nonsmoking B&B; any smokers in your party are welcome to sit out on the deck and enjoy the view.

Our normal check-in time is 4 P.M. to 9 P.M. Check-out time is 10 A.M.

We require at least ten days' notice from your check-in date to cancel your reservation and refund your deposit.

Please don't hesitate to call with any questions. We look forward to meeting you!

Magically yours,

Caroline Muir

Innkeeper

000 Turtle Lane,
Sullivan's Island, SC 00000
(000) 000-0000
www.gullcottagebb.com

Gull Cottage
Bed & Breakfast

A Seaside Cottage Out of Time

Welcome, Guest!

We're delighted to have you here at Gull Cottage, your home away from home on Sullivan's Island. Don't hesitate to ask for sightseeing and entertainment information—or for anything else we can do to make your stay memorable.

We've learned that most guests are concerned about the following items, so we've outlined them for you here:

- ○ *Smoking is not allowed in the house. If you'd like to light up, you're welcome to use the back deck.*

- ○ *Make yourself at home in the parlor, the Captain's study, and the dining room, as well as on the veranda and back deck. The kitchen is cook's territory only. If you'd like to stash cold drinks, picnic stuff, or restaurant doggy bags, you can use the guest fridge on the back porch.*

- ○ *Breakfast is served in the dining room from 8:00 to 9:30 each morning. If you're an early riser, you'll find coffee and tea on the dining room sideboard. Help yourself!*

- ○ *You'll find a telephone for your use in the Captain's study. Local calls are free. You'll need to use your credit card or calling card to place long-distance calls.*

- ○ *We love to arrange specially catered romantic or festive picnics on the beach and candlelit suppers for two served in your room. Ask to see our menu of delights and price list.*

- ○ *Take your house key as well as your room key when you go out. We may not be in when you get back, and we don't want you to be locked out.*

- ○ *Park your car in the gravel lot at the side of the house. If you park on the street, you could be towed away.*

- ○ *Check-out time is 10 A.M.*

Enjoy your stay!

Caroline Muir

and Nantucket, the cottage cat!

Reservations Calendar, The Secret Chamber, June 20xx

Sun.	Mon.	Tues.	Wed.	Thurs.	Fri.	Sat.
1 Vaint →→→	2	3	4	5	6 Blum ↑	7
8 Blum	9	10	11	12	13 Evans ↑	14
15 Evans	16	17	18	19	20 Clooney ↑	21
22 Clooney →→→ 23 Harr		24	25	26	27 ↑	28 Agnier →
29 Agnier →→→	30					

Reservations Calendar, Captain's Stateroom, June 20xx

Sun.	Mon.	Tues.	Wed.	Thurs.	Fri.	Sat.
1 Carter	2	3	4	5	6	7 Smythe
8 Smythe	9	10	11	12	13	14
15 Smythe	16	17	18 Gold	19	20	21
22 Gold	23 Chen	24	25	26	27	28 Porter
29 Porter	30					

Inn-Ternal Affairs
Employees
and Staff

Unless you start off as a small homestay and, by choice, don't grow your business, you'll find sooner or later that you need help. There's just too much to do to keep at it all on your own. You'll run out of energy and enthusiasm, and you'll burn out.

In this chapter, we'll explore when to hire help, how to find gem employees, and how to use them to your—and their—best advantage.

Helping Hands

Just when you'll need assistance depends on your energy level, the size of your operation, and your occupancy rate. But when exactly does the time come? "Probably your first day," advises Pat Hardy, formerly with the Professional Association of Innkeepers International (PAII). "No matter how many rooms you have, you need not be the room cleaner. As soon as you're just the room cleaner and don't have time to do marketing and to spend with guests, you begin to see a slide and deal with burnout."

Everybody, Pat says, needs to build some sort of relief into their business plan, whether it's an inn-sitter who takes over temporarily to give you a couple weeks off or a high school student who comes in to clean on weekends. "Innkeeping is a job that should not be 24/7, or you can't be fresh."

Thirty to 40 percent of all innkeepers don't employ any sort of staff, Pat explains. If you're a small operation, you may be able to work solo. But at five to six rooms, she says, you must look at employing a cleaning staff.

Of the five innkeeping couples we interviewed, only one does not have some sort of hired assistance. "Everything is done by the two of us," say Warrensburg, Missouri-based Bill and Sandra Wayne, who operate their two suites, the five-room farmhouse, and the cottage, all on their own.

David and Marilyn Lewis in Fort Worth, Texas, run their two cottages and three corporate units with the help of a contract cleaning lady. Steve and Nancy Sandstrom in Bayfield, Wisconsin, with five guest rooms and one suite, have one permanent part-time employee and one summer part-timer. Nancy and Charles Helsper in San Diego employ seven innkeepers (managers who act as hosts and oversee operations) and four housekeepers for their 12 guest rooms and suites. And Bruce and Judy Albert in Seaside, Florida, have ten multitasking employees for their seven rooms and two suites.

Many Tasks, Many Hats

While cleaning is often the first task for which you turn for help, it's certainly not the only one. If you're a clean machine who enjoys the cardiovascular crunch of whizzing around with a vacuum, dust rag, and sponge, but you hate number-crunching with a passion, you might find your employee dollars are better spent hiring a bookkeeper than a chamber maid. If you can command higher room revenues by sharing your expertise with your target market over a leisurely breakfast than rushing back and forth from the kitchen, then you might find it wise to hire a cook or kitchen helper.

Or go for a stellar multitasker who can pitch in and lend a hand with everything, as the Alberts in Seaside, Florida, have done. "The people who work for us are multitalented, from washing dishes, serving breakfast, cleaning rooms, answering the phone, and taking reservations to gardening and greeting and checking guests in and out," they explain. "They wear so many hats that it takes a special person."

You're the Boss

Employees can make your hosting duties easier and more fun, and can promote a sense of family for both you and your guests. But employees also mean increased responsibilities. Instead of flying solo—free of all the 9-to-5 world's rules and regulations—you find yourself with payroll to be met, workers' compensation insurance to purchase, and quarterly payroll taxes to file and pay.

Then you have to be able to delegate, which is easy for some people but extremely difficult for others. While you may be a people person when it comes to hosting guests, you'll learn that working with employees is entirely different. Being able to rule with a firm hand while allowing for creativity and individual personality quirks, encouraging independent action while instilling your own imprint on every task, is an art that takes practice and perseverance.

The Helspers have had the same head housekeeper for eight years. "She's the reason we're successful," Nancy says. "She really cares." The inn owners sit in when their housekeeper interviews potential employees but otherwise give her free rein. She does her own scheduling and manages her own staff.

The Sandstroms have also been lucky—and smart—in their choice of a housekeeper. She also tackles gardening and has used her artistic abilities stenciling the walls.

Going for the Gold

So where do you find the gold standard of employees? Start by deciding what you want done. If your primary goal is getting rooms cleaned, you'll look in different places than if you want a bookkeeper or marketing whiz. Try these tips for starters:

- *Teen talent*. High school and college kids make fine seasonal and part-time cleaning assistants. They're eager for work during spring and summer breaks, which may be the times of the year you need them most. This works out great because—unlike adults—they won't miss the income when the season, and their jobs, are over for the year. Place ads on school bulletin boards, go to school placement centers, or talk to career counselors.

- *Mom power*. Moms of school-age kids make great part-time employees. They like to work while the children are in school and be home in the afternoons, which makes them good candidates for morning chores like kitchen help and room cleaning. The best way to find moms is to ask around your neighborhood or place an ad on church or community center bulletin boards.

Smart Tip

When hiring innkeepers (managers who act as hosts and oversee operations), part time is better than full time, advises Nancy Helsper in San Diego. "Otherwise you burn people out," she says. "No one will do the job like you. It's better all around if they work four to six hours instead of eight."

- *Seniority surge.* Seniors may not have the stamina to run up and down stairs with cleaning caddies, but they make excellent assistants who can send out confirmation letters, address newsletters, answer the phone, and greet guests. Seniors are typically up with the birds (or earlier), so

they're good candidates for bustling about the kitchen at dawn, starting coffee and breakfast, and laying the table. And since their earnings from you may be supplemented by Social Security income, seniors generally don't mind working part time. Place ads on bulletin boards in church and senior centers, and put the word out to center staff.

- *The intern.* For creative efforts like designing and updating your web site, developing marketing materials, and writing articles and press releases, go back to school. Find a college student to take on your tasks as an intern. Interns generally work for a single season for a minimal salary or even for free in exchange for a learning experience and a terrific job to list on their resumes.

- *Outsource options.* Another option for almost any task is to hire an outside service. From cleaning and bookkeeping to gardening and pool maintenance to publicity, there's a company out there happy to come to your rescue. The advantage of this is that you don't have to worry about payroll, payroll taxes, or workers' compensation. The disadvantages are that you may pay more to a service than you would for an employee, and you may not get the same person each time, which means you'll have to go through an orientation/training session with each new face.

Stat Fact

Tourism equals jobs. According the American Hotel & Motel Association, tourism is the first, second, or third largest employer in 30 states and the third largest retail industry in the country.

What will you pay your employees—from kitchen helpers to housekeepers to inn-sitters? According to John Sheiry of the Distinguished Inns Alliance (which owns PAII), the answer to that question is entirely dependent on the going wages in your area and the experience level of the employee. A housekeeper in Napa, California, will generally command more money than one in, say, Fargo, North Dakota, or Panama City Beach, Florida. A good way to determine wage standards for your area is to look at the classifed ads in your local newspaper.

Sorority Sisters

Your employees often become extended family, which, like real family, has its ups and downs, as Nancy and Charles Helsper in San Diego learned. Not knowing where to turn when the manager they'd inherited with the inn left, they hired girls from Nancy's college sorority. The girls were all very cute and perky, Nancy says, but she and Charles soon became surrogate parents. Somebody was always short on her rent or had car problems, and "Mom and Dad" would feel compelled to fund a loan.

"They all went to the same sorority party on the same night," Nancy recalls. "At Christmas, they all kissed us on the cheeks and went home, leaving us to mind the inn for two or three weeks." Then the girls' school schedules changed every semester, necessitating complex schedule juggling at the inn.

After the perky sorority girls, Charles and Nancy hired and trained aspiring innkeepers, who had to commit to a year at the inn. A few left, deciding it was too much work. But on the whole, the system was a success. "It worked really well," Nancy says. "They had a passion for the business; they were living out their fantasies."

Still, having to hire new trainees each year became a problem. So what was the solution? "The best innkeepers are mature people who want a second career or a lifestyle change," Nancy says. Older people, she feels, tend to be more conscientious than younger ones who feel innkeeping is "just a job."

Home Help

The time-honored alternative to hiring employees is to turn to your family for innkeeping assistance. Depending on their age levels, kids can clean rooms, address envelopes, weed the garden, set the table, cook, answer the phone, and greet guests. Older kids often achieve guru level that adults can't match when it comes to computer tasks—give them your web site design or data entry duties, and let 'em roll.

Most kids enjoy helping out in the family business. And it's good for them—they learn the facts of financial life and the magic of meeting people—elements that will carry them farther than their peers at an earlier age. But don't force them if they're not inclined. Children mature toward different tasks at different ages. If yours just aren't ready emotionally or are into the let's-be-surly-and-rebellious mode, don't push them. It won't be good for you, your kids, or your guests.

Slammed by a Suitcase

Workers' compensation insurance covers you for any illness or injury your employees might incur on the job, from a back injury lifting luggage to a sprained ankle slipping on a snowy path to a case of contact dermatitis from a new cleaning product.

Even though employees are on the job in your home, your homeowner's insurance won't cover them because it's also your B&B and place of employment. So you must have separate coverage. Workers' compensation insurance laws vary from state to state; check with your insurance agent for details in your area.

Independents Days

If you opt for an outside service instead of employees, make sure you're hiring either a full-fledged company or a bona fide independent contractor—a term that confuses many an employer. People often think that anybody they pay to perform a part-time service on a casual basis is an independent contractor. Not. Or at least not according to the IRS.

Let's say you need somebody to clean guest rooms. You hire the nice lady down the street, who comes in three mornings a week or whenever you need her. You pay her a set fee per room, and you don't pay all those payroll taxes or workers' compensation insurance fees because she's an independent contractor.

This is a considerable savings. If you hired her as an employee, you'd also pay payroll taxes to the state and federal governments, and workers' compensation insurance in case she got injured in the line of duty.

But there's a major catch here. The IRS casts a very beady eye on the practice of hiring independent contractors because it believes employers are trying to cheat their way out of paying taxes. For a person to be considered an independent contractor and not an employee, she must meet the following requirements:

- Works for other bed and breakfasts or other companies besides yours
- Sets her own hours instead of you telling her when to report
- Comes ready-trained instead of you training her
- Can't be fired (although you can choose not to use her again after she finishes her current project)

Sitting Inn

Even if you've got the best employees in the world, you still need to get away once in a while. Innkeeping is labor-intensive as well as emotion-intensive work. You're "on" every minute you're in the B&B. And even if you've got living quarters at the back of the property instead of in the house proper, you'll still have one eye and one ear cocked on the business 24/7. It's fun, but it's also draining.

Fun Fact

In 1900, you could stay at the first-class Lenox Hotel—which featured shower baths and a roof garden—for prices starting at $2 per night.

"We try to take a significant vacation of a few weeks every April," Nancy Sandstrom in Wisconsin says. "We close two weeks for Christmas and New Year's, and we close for Easter. It's family time. We could get revenues during those periods, but family takes precedence."

If your business is seasonal, you may be able to shut down for a few weeks or more and get out of town on your own adventure, staying at other people's B&Bs. But if

Burn, Baby, Burn

Burnout is a serious problem in the B&B industry, mainly because hosts who are already wearing too many hats and burning the candle at both ends are so dedicated that they can't make themselves take a break. Just when an innkeeper reaches burnout depends on the individual, the level of planning that's gone into his operation, and the marketplace in which he's operating, says Pat Hardy formerly with the Professional Association of Innkeepers International. "Some people burn out the first week. Some pace themselves and burn out six or seven times during their careers," Hardy explains. "They go on vacation and come back renewed, or fix up a room and get recharged."

How many hosts flat-out burn up and give up? "Within the first five years, 25 to 30 percent will have said they don't like the job," Hardy says. "It's more disillusion than failure. We see very little failure—innkeepers may personally feel they've failed, but they don't go belly-up and file for bankruptcy. In the next five to ten years for that initial group, 25 to 30 percent will say 'I've done this; I've got places I want to go; I'm going to try something else.' In the next ten years, 25 to 40 percent are left. They may last a long time, depending on age and family status."

your business is steady—or you're working to make it steady—you can't afford to hang out the "Gone Fishin'" sign and take off. What's the solution?

Hire an inn-sitter, a baby-sitter for your B&B. Inn-sitters can be former hosts or managers who've gone on to other endeavors but still like to keep their hands on the bed and breakfast tiller once in a while, or hopeful hosts who've taken formal training but haven't yet found (or been able to afford) their dream B&B. Find an inn-sitter by contacting PAII or your local B&B association, or by checking the pages of industry publications.

As your operation grows, you may also want to hire an assistant innkeeper or manager to help handle the reins—and to fill in while you take that well-deserved vacation. A good assistant or manager can be worth his or her weight in silver-dollar pancakes, allowing you to not only take a break but devote your energies to marketing and promotions instead of day-to-day mini-crises.

Salaries for assistant hosts or managers vary with the size of the B&B, the demands of the job, and whether or not room-and-breakfast board are included. As a rough ballpark, expect to pay in the range of $1,000 to $3,000 per month.

Manual Labor

A policies and procedures manual is a smart way to insure that employees and inn-sitters know how you like things done. You don't have to write a 300-page instruction book that reads like a General Accounting Office report—a brief description of every-day tasks is fine.

Start with a three-ring binder, and put each page in a plastic or cellophane sleeve. Make up pages for policies and procedures including the following:

- *Reservations*. This can consist of the same materials you keep at your reservations center: your room rates, deposits, cancellation and refund policy, and even a script for how to answer the phone. Make sure to put in a sample confirmation letter.

- *Check-in and check-out*. Describe your check-in and check-out routines and policies.

- *Cleaning*. Write out exactly what needs to be cleaned in each guest room and any specific instructions like "Empty wastebaskets and wipe down with green disinfectant, then put in new liner." Or "Don't use window cleaner on antique mirror. Wipe gently with damp cloth." Do the same for the kitchen, common rooms, and exterior areas like verandas and porches.

- *Breakfasts*. Describe your serving schedule(s), whether you deliver coffee to rooms or set it on the sideboard, etc. Add

> ### Fun Fact
> Want a chicken salad at four in the morning? In 1969, Westin Hotels & Resorts became the first chain to offer 24-hour room service.

in a week or two's worth of recipes with any special preparation tips.

- *Guest relations.* Write out tips on how to handle common guest questions or problems, from gently but firmly reprimanding smokers on not smoking indoors to the complaining guest to the one who wants to see inside the carriage house—which happens to be your private quarters. If the house has a special history that guests ask about, write that out as well.

- *Emergencies.* Put in emergency phone numbers, everything from the fire department and the septic service to the plumber and the bakery that supplies your morning croissants.

Choosing the Best

Taking on an employee—whether a part-time chamber person to clean rooms or a full-time assistant innkeeper—can be nerve-wracking, on a par with leaving your baby with a sitter for the first time. How do you choose somebody who can be a back up to you, who can nurture your business and your guests the way you do?

It's simple, really, once you narrow it down to manageable steps. Start with the following four tasks:

1. *Write out a job description.* Start with a paragraph or two describing the tasks to be performed and the skills needed. Will you want your new employee to come in for six hours every Saturday and clean guest rooms? Spend four mornings a week sending confirmations and answering the phone? Or work eight hours a day June through August at cleaning, gardening, cooking, and greeting guests right along with you?

2. *Identify the personality traits needed for the job.* Do you need a methodical, detail-oriented type to track your reservations, confirmations, and deposits, and handle all the bookkeeping or a bouncy go-getter who can entertain children one hour, host a tea the next, and change the belt on the vacuum cleaner in between?

3. *Consider your own personality and the needs of the job.* If you're a perky, cheerful person who's rarin' to go at 6 A.M., you'll have a rough go with an employee who never says a word before 9 A.M. But if you conk out at 8 P.M., that night owl employee might be just the one to wait up for late-arriving guests

Stat Fact
According to the American Hotel & Lodging Association, at most recent count the country's lodging industry encompassed 47,590 properties with 4.4 million rooms and $122.7 billion in sales.

List the 10 or 12 skills or qualities you want most, rank them, and circle the essential three or four. You might, for instance, consider honesty—essential when employees will have access to guest rooms and luggage; friendliness—for meeting and greeting guests; or computer smarts—for entering data or working on your web site.

Advertising for Expertise

Now craft a classified ad to place in the local newspaper, various B&B publications, or post on college, church, or senior center bulletin boards, depending on what sort of help you're seeking. Make your ad clear, clean, and brief—but also make the job sound as interesting as possible. Take a look at the sample below:

Assistant Needed

Historic bed and breakfast on beach needs talented summer assistant to greet guests, help with breakfasts, housekeeping, and reservations. Must be a cheerful, computer-literate self-starter. You'll work hard but have fun, too. Send resume to
P.O. Box 917,
Sullivan's Island, SC 00000.

Note that the ad instructs applicants to mail in a resume. You'll eliminate a lot of people who lack follow-through by the simple fact that they won't bother to send anything in, and you can eliminate a lot more who would like the position but are unqualified. Of course, if you're looking for high schoolers to do part-time cleaning, you'll do better to ask applicants to call—they probably won't have a resume to send.

Inn-Terview Basics

After you've weeded out the applicants who don't seem qualified, call in each of your best candidates for an individual interview. To start the interview process, briefly describe your B&B and the position available. Establish a rapport.

Then focus your questions by asking about several general areas—work-related experience, training, lifestyle (hobbies and related interests), then education and unrelated jobs. Move into each area with an open-ended statement like "Tell me about your last job." Don't be specific—you want to know what the applicant considers important. If you're talking to high schoolers or college kids—people who may not have previous work histories—ask about school projects that will relate (when interviewing interns, for instance) or about odd jobs or fund-raisers they may have done.

The Building Super

One of the givens of the lodging industry is that there's always some sort of maintenance and repair to be done. Clogged toilets, sinks that don't drain, floors that creak and windows that leak, circuits that short out, heaters that don't heat, vacuum cleaners that quit … the list goes on and on. You can call out a repair service for each and every one of these mini-disasters. But this gets expensive fast, and the repairperson doesn't always show up when you need him.

So it's smart to become your own building superintendent. If you don't know how to do the handyperson thing, learn. Home improvement stores often offer free classes on everything from installing toilets to building decks. Sign up for these. Purchase a few DIY (do-it-yourself) books. Watch fix-it shows on *Home & Garden TV* and *The Learning Channel*. You'll soon be a pro.

When you have information on which to base further questions, ask what the applicant liked or disliked about a specific aspect of a job he's described. When you ask what sort of problems arose and how your candidate handled them, you'll pick up tips on whether he approached challenges with initiative or by asking for help.

Ask other questions like: What was most challenging about . . .? What were your major accomplishments in . . . and why? Is there anything you regret about . . .? What did you learn from . . . that might help you in this position?

Pace your interview to leave time to discuss the open position in detail. It's not only what you ask the candidate but what he asks you that can be revealing.

When you identify the best interviewee, call his references—check that he's the good right hand you think he is. Then call to tell him the good news. Also call or write the candidates you didn't choose. Thank them for their time, and let them know you'll keep their applications on file in case another position opens. This is not only courteous but gives you a head start the next time you need help.

Booking Up
Advertising and Marketing

You can't rely on walk-in traffic to fill your rooms. Most guests will want to make reservations long before they actually arrive on your doorstep. And since they'll be coming from points all over the country or even the globe, this means they won't even know you exist—and therefore won't be able to book a room with you—unless you advertise. So advertising and marketing are a tremendously important part of your job.

Promoting your B&B takes time, effort, and creativity. But if you do the job right, the payoff is well worth the work.

In this chapter we'll explore the elements of bed and breakfast advertising and marketing, from print ads and press releases to direct mail and publicity ploys. You'll learn what it takes to attract tourists and travelers and turn them into guests.

Getting Acquainted

The first thing to do when you start your advertising and marketing campaign is to revisit your market research and reacquaint yourself with your target market. Ask yourself these questions one more time:

- Who are my potential guests? (honeymooners and other romantics, families, business travelers, hikers, bike enthusiasts, or some other group entirely?)
- How many are there?
- Where are they located?
- Where do they now find the lodging accommodation I want to provide?
- What can I offer at my bed and breakfast that they're not already getting from this other source?
- How can I persuade them to stay at my bed and breakfast?

Look over the answers to these questions, then ask yourself some more:

- What image do I want to project?
- How do I compare with my competition, and how can I be better?

After you've answered these questions you can start planning your strategy and the type of advertising you'll do.

Mail Rooms

Direct mail can be one of the innkeeper's best tools. It gives you the ability to sell to those potential guests all over the country, or all over the world if you choose, whether your B&B is nestled beside the sea in Maine, deep in the California desert, tucked away in the Hill Country of Texas, or anyplace else.

Direct mail also lets you target the specific market you want to attract. Because you send your sales piece right into the post boxes of people with a proven interest in travel and touring, you eliminate the problem of spending expensive advertising dollars on people who don't like to travel or can't afford it. And if you're targeting a specific niche, like history buffs, hiking enthusiasts, or romance readers or writers, you can zero in on that specific market.

The Guest List

So where do you find all those tourists and travelers? As we briefly explored in our market research phase in Chapter 3, you've got several sources:

- Rosters and directories from clubs, civic and professional organizations, non-profit associations, or other groups
- List brokers
- Your own in-house lists

Rousting Up Rosters

You may already belong to a group that's the perfect target market for your bed and breakfast. For instance, a bird-watching group whose members will thrill to your proximity to bird habitats, a gardening club whose members will delight in your inn's heirloom flower garden, or a parents' group from the PTA to home school associations to Mothers of Twins for your kid-friendly service. If your organization is a local one, that's great. But if it has regional or national chapters, so much the better. More names!

If your B&B will target a more general market, like couples seeking a romantic weekend, then you might start off with any associations you belong to, be they car club, pony club, quilters' guild, weight-loss group, or teachers' league.

The point is that you've probably got a membership directory tucked away in a desk file or buried beneath all those supermarket coupons in your kitchen catch-all drawer. If not, you may be able to beg, borrow, or buy a directory from the organization's main office.

Brainstorm any other associations whose membership rosters you may be able to get access to, including those of your spouse or significant other; your siblings, parents and children; and any other friends or relatives who might be willing to contribute a mailing list.

Consider church groups, client lists, employee directories, neighborhood groups, fraternal organizations like the Elks Lodge, alumni associations, and sororities and fraternities. And don't neglect your own address book—you've probably got far more names and addresses scribbled in there than you realize.

Going for Brokers

Perhaps one of the best sources of mailing lists is the list broker, a a company whose only business is developing and renting lists of names and addresses. List brokers can

What's In a Name?

As an added bonus to compiling your own mailing list, you can make money with it without booking a single room. You do this by offering your list through a broker in exchange for a commission, usually about 20 percent of your rental fee. So if you charge the going rate of $50 per thousand names and a specialty travel company, for instance, buys 10,000 names, you earn $500. Pay the broker a $100 commission and the other $400 is yours!

supply you with lists for just about every niche imaginable—tourists and business travelers, retirees, parents, cooks, gardeners, bicycling enthusiasts, nature lovers, history buffs, and much, much more.

Even better, a good list broker can pull together just about any specific criteria, or selects, to best target your special market. Say your niche is outdoors-oriented families. Your market research has shown that college-educated parents with a household income of over $60,000 per year are the most likely to stay at your B&B. And you want to start your sales blitz on a relatively small scale by sending brochures to potential guests in your own part of your state instead of nationwide. So you request a list in which all the names are college-educated parents of preteen kids with annual household incomes of $60,000-plus who live in upstate New York.

Where does the list broker get all these names? All sorts of sources, including magazine subscriptions, the cards you fill out and mail in when you register a new piece of software or a new refrigerator, financial ratings lists, rosters of political and professional organizations, and the customer lists of companies that sell by mail order.

The Price of Selects

Mailing lists don't come cheap. Costs vary depending on how many selects you request and whether you spring for a compiled or response list—the latter is more specific and therefore more expensive. A compiled list might be composed of people who subscribe to gardening magazines, while a response list would be comprised of people who not only subscribe to gardening magazines and earn more than $50,000 annually but have also booked room reservations in the past six months. This is important, because it tells you that they're much more likely to reserve a stay with you than to throw out your brochure along with yesterday's paper.

Expect to pay about $50 per 1,000 names for a compiled list and as much as $120 per 1,000 names for the response list, plus $5 to $10 extra for each select—like age, income, or geographic region—that you request. And list brokers generally demand that you rent at least 3,000 to 5,000 names at a time.

We say "rent" instead of "purchase" because you only get to use each list once—if you want to use it again, you pay another rental fee. However, any names who respond to your mailing are yours to keep and reuse as often as you like absolutely free.

The House List

This brings us to the third option for finding direct-mail customers: your own in-house list. You should begin developing a mailing list at about the same time you start developing your B&B—it's never too early to start. Try these tips for building your own list:

- Use the names you receive in response to your market research surveys.
- Develop a database of all guests' names and addresses. Most B&B software will do this for you; if you don't purchase industry-specific software, buy a mailing list program, or keep a written log.
- Keep a book with spaces for nonguest visitors to record their names and addresses. Ask people to write in it when you host your grand opening party as well as any other public relations events.
- Swap lists with other innkeepers, either on a one-time or permanent basis. This may sound like a case of cutting your own throat by sharing your hard-won guests, but it's not. B&B guests like to sample lots of different inns, so they'll probably shop around anyway. And if yours shines by comparison, they'll come back to you.

While you're cheerily adding these names to your list, you'll also want to go to the trouble of maintaining it. Make sure you've got each name entered only once—sending duplicate brochures or other materials not only looks unprofessional but is also a serious waste of money. Weed out any return-to-sender names and edit any who notify you of new addresses. Make sure, too, that you've entered all names and addresses correctly into your database. Nobody likes to get a piece of mail with his name spelled wrong, and sending mail to a nonexistent address is pound- and penny-foolish.

Brochures and Other Brilliance

No mailing list, no matter how well-targeted, is going to do a lick of good if you don't have a brochure or other sales materials that get out there and sell your B&B's special brand of character and ambience. You may want to send out periodic sales letters, postcards, or newsletters. But the most common "salesman" for the bed and breakfast is the brochure, so we'll start with it.

▲

A B&B brochure is typically printed on both sides of a sheet of 8.5-by-11-inch paper and then folded in thirds. This works well for several reasons:

- It's the perfect size to slip into a regular No. 10 business-sized envelope along with a sales letter.

- It's a relatively inexpensive route to go because it doesn't call for any oddball-size paper that a print shop will have to special-order or cut to size.

Smart Tip

Tip...

Instead of printing your rates on your brochure, print them up on a one-page insert. It's far less expensive to reprint the rate sheet or card than to reprint the whole brochure.

- It fits tidily into the brochure racks at tourist information and visitor centers.

But since the letter-size brochure is exactly the same size as everybody else's, it means you'll have to exercise that creativity to make yours stand out from the crowd. The best way to start is to examine the brochures of every other bed and breakfast, country inn, and similarly targeted hotel you can get your hands on. Note what you like and dislike about each, what works and what doesn't, and then design your own accordingly.

Some industry experts recommend going with a four-color extravaganza that shows off your B&B's stunning exterior on the front page with perhaps a few thumbnail

---

Sweet Rolls for Remembrance

Take a healthy handful of your brochures to your local tourist or visitors center and convention bureau as well as those of outlying areas whose visitors may be traveling in your direction. Pay frequent visits to replenish your stock—but don't be a drop and run. Take a moment to chat up the staff. Tell them about your B&B; bring along a plate of your famous cookies or sweet rolls. The more they know about your inn, and the more fondly they think of you, the better your chances for referrals

"I take brochures to convention and visitors bureaus in four different locations," says Marilyn Lewis in Fort Worth, Texas. "I take little personalized cookies as well. When I go around, I help people like me as well. They remember!"

While making your rounds, leave brochures and cookies at your chamber of commerce. Check out the lobbies of restaurants and attractions—they often have racks in which you can place your brochures. Just ask permission first so you don't step on any toes.

photos of guest rooms on the inside. Others avow that this is a waste of money and suggest you go with an evocative line drawing or two by a local artist instead. The choice is yours—go with the style that suits your inn and its ambience.

What you say in your brochure should also reflect the character of your bed and breakfast. But go sparingly with the flowery prose. It's easy to get carried away with adjectives like "charming," "quaint," "historic," and "romantic." But remember, every other B&B is probably using exactly the same words over and over again—so try to find other, better, ways to say the same thing. Create word pictures. Instead of romantic, for instance, you might say something like "starry nights to remember" or "a sea-kissed weekend you'll treasure." Instead of "charming," how about "captivating," "enchanting," or "bewitching?"

Along with the creative writing, what elements should you include in your brochure?

- A description of your B&B and its ambience—try something such as "A jewel-box bed and breakfast and a garden-lover's paradise, nestled in three acres of heirloom flowers and herbs." Or "The lakeside vacations you remember from childhood all grown-up. Idyllic views, sensuous decor, and fresh blueberries for breakfast."

- Your address, phone number, toll-free number, and web address. Don't make it hard for prospective guests to figure out how to contact you for reservations.

- Your rates, which can also be called tariffs. It's fun for guests (and you) if you give each room or suite a name. Providing a brief description of each room along with its price also makes the whole price thing more fun and tantalizing. Think of your rates as a sort of B&B version of a menu. "The Queen Bee: Corner room with views of city lights and queen sleigh bed" sounds more interesting than "Queen bed room."

- What your rates include (for instance, gourmet breakfast and afternoon tea, continental breakfast and a one-day ski pass, or simply breakfast)

- If you have any special rate policies such as two-night minimums

- Your deposit, cancellation, and refund policies

- Your check-in and check-out times

- Your payment policies (whether you accept American Express, MasterCard, Visa, or personal checks)

- Your policies on smoking, pets, and children

- Brief description of special packages for weddings, business conferences, and private parties

- Endorsements from magazine or other reviewers or glowing testimonials from satisfied guests

- A map showing your location from state and interstate highways

- Brief description of area sights and attractions

This is a lot to pack into one small brochure, so keep it simple. Tantalize and tempt, enough so prospective guests will call for more information and then make reservations. But don't try to cram every single thing you can think of into one brochure—too much information in a small space is messy and hard to read rather than intriguing. Take a look at the sample policy statement and rate sheet on page 189 for an idea of how to word your own.

Savoir Sales Letters

People will read and heed unsolicited letters—when written well—more than they will an unaccompanied brochure. You'll want to include a sales letter as part of your direct-mail campaign—take a look at the sample on page 193. While just what you say will depend on your target market, you can follow these tips for savoir-faire:

- *Write as though you're sending a personal note to one special guest—not as if you're sending the same message to everyone on your mailing list (even though you are).* Let your enthusiasm for your B&B shine through.

- *Don't skimp on words.* Surprisingly, even though people complain about the profusion of "junk" mail they receive, longer sells better than shorter. Potential guests are interested in what you're selling, either because they're confirmed B&B junkies, gardening fiends, nature-lovers, businesses seeking conference retreats, or whatever. So indulge their interests—tell them all about your gardens, your gourmet meals, your proximity to nature, or whatever your hook is.

- *Use indented paragraphs, boldface type, italics, underlined words, and two colors—they pack more of a punch.* But use them sparingly. Overused, like those cutesy adjectives, they lose their appeal and become downright annoying.

- *Make sure all spelling, grammar, and punctuation is perfect.* Even if you're a former high school English teacher, have a trusted colleague or relative look over your materials. You could miss a glaring typo merely by having read it twice too often.

Pillow Talk

Two of your most effective direct-mail tools are the endorsement and the testimonial, seductive phrases about your pillows—and beds and breakfasts—from other people. If you say, "My inn is the best in the state," prospective guests will take it with several grains of salt. It's your inn, so of course you'll sing its praises. But if impartial third parties say your inn is the best in the state, readers will believe it.

Endorsements are the best pillow talk but also the hardest to get. These are quotes from media people—magazines, newspapers, or TV reporters—but can also be favorable reviews from big names recognizable to your target market. If you'll give gourmet

Policy Statement

◆ Our room rates are based on double occupancy (two people), and do not include sales and occupancy taxes. They do include Jan's mouth-watering home-baked breakfasts.

◆ We can accommodate a third guest on a rollaway bed in our larger rooms for an additional $20 per night.

◆ We have a two-night minimum for weekend stays and four-night minimums for selected holidays and special events. Please ask when you make your reservation.

◆ Check-in time is 4 P.M.; check-out is 11 A.M. Please note that we're on Central Time.

◆ For all reservations, we require a 50 percent deposit with the balance due on your arrival.

◆ We accept MasterCard, Visa, cash, and personal checks.

◆ Cancellations must be received at least 14 days prior to arrival date, or we cannot refund your deposit.

◆ We cannot provide refunds for early departures.

◆ Pieces of Eight is a smoke-free B&B.

◆ We cannot accept pets—if you're traveling with Boots or Fido, we'll be happy to recommend a nearby pet hotel.

Gull Cottage
Bed & Breakfast
A Seaside Cottage Out of Time

Gull Cottage
Bed & Breakfast

A Seaside Cottage Out of Time

Our Room Rates

The Captain's Stateroom
King bed, private balcony overlooking the sea
$100/night March thru August
$50/night September thru February

The Smugglers' Chamber
King bed, private balcony overlooking the sea
$100/night March thru August
$50/night September thru February

The Secret Chamber
Queen bed in a tower room
$85/night March thru August
$42.50/night September thru February

The Pirate's Lady's Chamber
Queen bed overlooking the garden
$85/night March thru August
$42.50/night September thru February

---

*All rooms feature private baths, televisions, VCRs,
and ceiling fans to stir our intoxicating sea air.*

Just a little taste of your balcony view...

Smart Tip

Send former guests short surveys, and then ask to use the most favorable and interesting answers as testimonials.

cooking workshops on selected weekends, for instance, you couldn't go wrong with an endorsement from famous chef Wolfgang Puck. We'll explore working with the media to get those endorsements on page 201.

Testimonials are quotes from previous guests—things like, "We celebrated our second anniversary at Gull Cottage. From the fresh roses in our room to the picnic breakfast on the beach, it was even more romantic than our honeymoon. Thank you, Mrs. Muir!"

How do you get testimonials? The best place is the guest book you'll set out in the parlor or other common room. Ask guests if you can use their words of praise in your promotional materials. Most people are delighted to be asked and will readily agree. You can also use complimentary comments from guests' e-mails and even phone calls—just be sure to ask for permission to use them. Keep in mind that it's illegal to use testimonials without permission. Also, always use real first and last names and real hometowns. If you put something like "I'll never stay anywhere else!" –Mrs. C., New York, the accolade looks phony even if it isn't.

Wish You Were Here

The brochure and sales letter are probably your best bets as far as soliciting business from people who haven't stayed with you yet. But they aren't the only ways to go with direct-mail sales materials. You've got lots of options; your own creativity is the only limit.

The following ideas typically work best when sent to previous guests or to people who've inquired about your B&B. But it doesn't necessarily mean you can't send them out to cold (or unsolicited) inquiries. Use your imagination, and modify them to suit your target market. Depending on the size of your mailings, you can craft and produce these with your own desktop-publishing software and printer. Or make up dummies, and have a local print shop do the printing. Start your brainstorming with these suggestions:

- *Newsletters.* Write and mail (or e-mail) quarterly newsletters. Describe seasonal changes in your garden, on the beach, or the ski slopes, give recipes from your kitchen, and share stories about new renovations or decor. Be sure to describe—in advance—any special events in your area that guests may want to attend or your own special promotions like a romantic Valentine's weekend, Christmas gala, or Fourth of July blast. Match the tone of your newsletter to the character of your B&B—whimsical, folksy, or breezy. But write it as if you're writing to friends and family—not stuffy or dull. Enliven it with humor.

And if you can't think of anything interesting to say, keep your prose short and fill empty spaces with line drawings or pertinent quotations.

- *Postcards*. Create your own "wish you were here" postcards by reproducing a photo of your B&B or a scenic view from your porch on card stock. Fill in the back with clever patter about your inn and an invitation to reserve a room for the coming season. People tend to read postcards that land in their mailboxes right away while other types of mail get tossed into the "sort later" stack.

> **Bright Idea**
> Stock writing desks in guest and common rooms with your postcards. Guests will send them to friends and relatives—and at the same time help you advertise your property.

- *Invitations*. Another piece of mail that people open immediately: invitations. They make a terrific reminder to book a room for a vacation, holiday, or other event. Use oversized envelopes that stand out from the rest of the chaff in the mailbox.

- *Cards*. If you track guests' birthdays and anniversaries, send out cards offering best wishes on the commemorative events. These are a thoughtful touch and, used wisely, can also serve as subtle nudges to book a room. Don't forget about other guest events like family reunions or annual girlfriend get-togethers that guests have celebrated with you in the past.

(Inter)Net Yourself a Guest

Perhaps your most important advertising tool is your web site. "It's tremendously important to advertise on the internet; it's the best form of advertising," advises Jerry Phillips, former executive director of the Professional Association of Innkeepers International. "A new B&B will get 95 percent of its guests from the net." And indeed, every one of the innkeepers we interviewed felt that advertising on the web was their top advertising venue.

Even if you go with a reservation service, you'll need a web site to give prospective guests an up-close-and-personal view of your inn, and let them sample your special brand of B&B ambience. You can attract more guests for far less money with a web site than with any other advertising venue. People all over the country and the world can visit your site, read your captivating descriptions, and view photos of your house, your guest rooms, your views, and even your resident cat or dog.

Basically, you can't afford not to have a web site. Merely putting one up, of course, isn't everything. Your web site needs to contain all the information in your brochure. Add more if you like, but follow the same rules: More isn't necessarily better unless it's visually appealing, entertaining, and informative.

Sales Letter

Gull Cottage Bed & Breakfast

A Seaside Cottage Out of Time

March 2, 20xx

Ms. Sydney Forsythe
Director of Human Relations
The Gadsden Company
1 Gadsden Square
Columbia, SC 20000

Dear Ms. Forsythe:

Your staff works hard for your company. You know how important it is to reward them for a job well done or to offer incentives to get that job done. A trip to Gull Cottage Bed & Breakfast is the perfect choice. Located on picture-perfect Sullivan's Island, just over the bridge from Charleston, South Carolina, we're only a few hours' drive from your offices. You don't have to factor in expensive air fares and extra travel time away from work.

More than that, your employees—and you, too!—will be eager to visit Gull Cottage, an enchanting seaside Victorian cottage built by a seafaring captain in 1886. Our doors and windows open right onto the beach, with all the magic of surf, sand, and sea air. We provide the ultimate bed and breakfast experience: gourmet home-cooked breakfasts and shore-side picnic lunches, fireplaces and whirlpool tubs in each room, and delightful decor from days gone by.

Imagine your arrival: The moment you emerge from your car, you sense the sea—the sensuous silky feel of salt air on your skin and the sound of the surf. Step through Gull Cottage's welcoming front door and into our cool, flower-filled parlor. My staff and I will greet you and show you to your room. You can kick back on the king-size bed and relax, or come down to the back veranda, which is right on the beach, for iced tea and delectable refreshments.

Spend the afternoon swimming, beachcombing, or just lazing in the sun. In the evening, choose from one of Charleston's many award-winning restaurants, and stroll the lamplit strees, peering into the city's secret gardens and admiring its

Sales Letter, continued

elegant, old-world homes. You may choose to return the next day for sightseeing, a ride in a horsedrawn carriage, antiquing, or touring nearby plantations.

Head back to the beach for more fun in the sun. Charter a boat—there's always a braggable catch to be had in our plentiful waters. Or snuggle up in a wicker chair on the veranda with a book from our Captain's Library. If you're lucky, you may catch a glimpse of the Captain himself—always considered a sign of good fortune by our guests.

Then there's our home-cooked breakfasts, served on the veranda in fine weather, to savor along with our heavenly special-blend coffee, and to anticipate each morning. If you like, we'll also provide a picnic basket packed with gourmet goodies so you don't have to leave the beach even to eat lunch.

Gull Cottage's guest rooms are havens of rest and relaxation. All open onto the sea or the garden and are filled with treasures brought back from the Captain's many voyages. Enjoy a fire in your own private hearth, a deep, soothing soak in your private whirlpool tub, and a restful night as the rhythm of the surf lulls you to sleep.

I used to work in the corporate world myself before I purchased and restored Gull Cottage. I know how important it is to take time out, time away to rest, rejuvenate, and restore your body, mind, and soul. That's why I'm so excited about sharing Gull Cottage with you and your staff.

And that's why I'm offering you a very special introductory corporate rate. Call or e-mail me for more information. Together, we'll put together a package custom-tailored to your company's needs.

Magically yours,

Caroline Muir

P.S. Gull Cottage is also a wonderful site for business conferences and retreats. Our small size allows us to give your needs our undivided attention. We'll provide everything from an overhead projector to faxing and copying services to gourmet goodies to help stir those creative juices. Forget the dull hotel decor and mass-produced meals—let us show you and your staff brainstorming the way it should be!

000 Turtle Lane,
Sullivan's Island, SC 00000
(000) 000-0000
www.gullcottagebb.com

If you are not extensively savvy in the computer department, you may want to have a web designer do your site for you. There is typically an overall design charge and then a charge for monthly (or however often you agree on) updates. The origination of the web site will probably cost a minimum of $1000; and you will still need to provide them with all of the information they need as well as photos.

Some tips for web design and implementation success include:

- Make the important information—your e-mail address and phone number—easy to find. Don't force guests to wade through page after page before locating them. Put contact information on your home page and on every other information page of your site.

- Design the site to keep viewers at your web site (known as "stickiness") instead of popping off to another site. You won't need to change your site frequently like retail sites need to do to keep customers coming back and finding new and interesting stuff. You may want to update it quarterly or even just annually—however often it takes to not be showing incorrect information or to promote seasonal specials or events.

- Do include all the information you would put in a well-designed brochure—and offer to send that brochure to anyone who wants one. This is a great way to add to your mailing (or e-mailing) list. And unlike a web site that needs to be actively searched, a brochure can be stuck on the refrigerator and entice the tired potential guest at the end of a long hard work week.

- Include things like whether your establishment is handicap accessible, whether you can/do accommodate food allergies, or any other way you go out of your way to make people comfortable and enjoy their stay. Guests to your site will use this info to compare to other bed and breakfast sites they come across.

- Just like you would with a print brochure, make sure the design of your web site reflects the style and flavor of your B&B. Don't use art deco styling for a B&B that is stately, elegant, and formal. Don't use black backgrounds with gold type and portray a formal look for a country style bed & breakfast. People who have never been to your establishment want to know the atmosphere they are checking themselves into.

- Include helpful and enticing links on your site, like to local shopping areas, restaurants, and major attractions.

- Definitely show photos of rooms on your site. If every room is worth a photo, great—you can provide a page of "thumbnails" that can be clicked on to be viewed in larger format.

- Like with your brochure, include glowing testimonials from guests. Enlarge one on each page of your web site to remind potential guests that real people have had thoroughly enjoyable stays at your establishment.

- Likewise, include any awards your bed and breakfast has won. If these awards are presented by interesting organizations, include links to those sites.

- If you sell cookbooks or antiques or mugs, T-shirts, and such, and you want to add a selling feature to your site, these would be great things to put on the site.

> ## Smart Tip
> Tip...
>
> Check out competitors' web sites just as you check out competitors' other advertising materials. Borrow the best of what they're doing, and then do it better.

- Make sure your site loads quickly and is easy to navigate. Add as many photos as you like, but don't make them so big that potential guests must wait eons to view them.

- Finally, put the site up only when it is complete, not with a bunch of "under construction" pages.

Guests can contact you for more information by e-mail with a single mouse click—which in itself is a powerful lure. It doesn't cost them any money in toll calls, and they can do it 24/7. Most people start "window shopping" for vacations late at night or in the wee hours of the morning. With e-mail, they can fire off a query to you—or even make a reservation—immediately. They don't have to wait until business hours, so the risk that they'll forget, lose interest, or lose your phone number is eliminated.

Check and answer your e-mail several times a day. The faster you respond, the more likely you are to get bookings. If guests leave a phone number, call them instead of e-mailing a response. Your friendly voice will garner more reservations than an e-answer because you can field questions guests will only think to ask once you're on the phone. And better yet, you can subtly sell at the same time.

Surfing Sites

Once you've got a web site, you're only halfway there. You now have to ensure that potential guests will find it. If no one's ever heard of you, they're not likely to get on the internet and type in your name. And you can't rely on major search engines like Yahoo!; there's no way they can keep up with the zillions of submissions they get every day.

This means you need to list your site with "guidebook" sites to which those prospective guests will go. People looking for a bed and breakfast in Florida, for instance, will probably go to Yahoo! or some other search engine, and type in "bed and breakfast, Florida." Duh. Of course. But this will bring up lots of guidebook sites, from www.floridainns.com (the Florida Bed & Breakfast Inns Association) to www.bbonline.com (Bed & Breakfast Inns Online) to www.bedandbreakfast.com (Bed and Breakfast.com). And if you're listed on those sites, guests can find you.

Prices for a listing on sites like these typically range from $100 to $500 per year, and include links to your own web site—which is important. Before signing on, surf through member listings. Do they appear similar in tone to your B&B? You don't want them to be clones of your ambience and style (because, after all, they'll be your direct competition), but you don't want to go with a site whose other listings are all motels or impersonal vacation condos, either. Ask the site owners for references; then check them. How much traffic has the site brought other innkeepers? How long have they been listed? What is their overall opinion of the site?

Going by the Guidebook

In years past, B&B hosts found that one of their best advertising venues was hard-copy guidebooks like the AAA Guide to Bed & Breakfasts in North America and The Unofficial Guide to Bed & Breakfasts in the Southeast. You sent your best blurb to the author and prayed that you'd be included. Then you'd wait up to a year for the next edition, hopefully showcasing your property, to appear on bookstore shelves.

Today, there are still scads of these B&B guidebooks available, but—thanks to the net—they're not anywhere near as important to the innkeeper as they once were. "We have been in a number of print guidebooks, which are hardly worth the bother any more," say Bill and Sandra Wayne in Warrensburg, Missouri. "State association guides and web sites have provided steady business."

Ruth Young of Mi Casa Su Casa reservation service organization (RSO) agrees that the internet is taking over a lot of the marketing work that print guides used to provide, but guidebooks are still a useful tool. "We are making the large majority of our bookings through the net," she says, but people are not just finding us by doing a web

Picture This

Get creative and think up promotional adjuncts to your web site. David and Marilyn Lewis in Fort Worth, Texas, take a photo of each set of guests, whether honeymooners or sisters on a girls' weekend out. Then, after getting guests' written permission, they post the photos on their web site. Guests can look up their own photos, e-mail them to friends and family, and even add them as screensavers to their computers with a click of a mouse.

Which is all fabulous free advertising. Each time guests—and their families and friends—go online, it's a fond memory and a persuasion to return, or a "Gee, let's go there ourselves" enticement to visit.

search," Young advises. "Future guests buy guidebooks that include our e-mail address and web address in our descriptions. I think guidebooks will continue to be very important in the near future."

If you'd like a guidebook listing, follow these steps:

- Go to your local or online bookseller and choose the guides you think your property will best fit into according to your location and target market.

- Put on your PR hat, and send a package to the book's author in care of the publisher. This package should include a personal letter in which you glowingly describe your B&B, its amenities, and nearby sights and attractions. Just as in your brochure and web site, keep it concise and full of character, and avoid those overused adjectives in favor of word pictures. With the letter, include your brochure and copies of any articles about your inn from other publications.

- Offer the writer a complimentary night at your B&B. Most authors don't visit the inns they cover, but some may take you up on it. One free night is well worth the paid room nights your listing may bring in.

- Most guidebook listings are free. However, if the author or publisher asks you to pay for your listing, do some more homework before agreeing. Ask around at PAII, your RSO, and your local association to find out whether other innkeepers have found the guidebook's listings to be a boon.

- Most state and regional associations provide guidebooks that list their members free of charge. Check with your association for details.

Breakfast Ads

Print ads, the ones you find in newspapers and magazines, are not the cheapest way to promote your bed and breakfast, but they can be effective—if you use them wisely. You must, first and foremost, decide if your target market is regional or national.

If you feel your target market includes people all over the country, you might want to advertise in a national publication such as Country Living. The upside to these ads is that hundreds of thousands of potential guests will see your ad. The downside is that a display ad—the kind with graphics—can run as high as $1,750 a pop. One way to get around this is to advertise in a regional edition of the same magazine, targeting, for

Smart Tip

Tip...

List your site on the Professional Association of Innkeepers International's Innplace.com—it's free to members. Also list your site with any local or regional associations to which you belong.

instance, readers in the Southeast or Northwest. This can help you reach a narrower target market while still going with a big-name national publication, and ad prices will be lower.

Even so, advertising in national publications is not usually the best bet for the B&B. Unlike direct-mail advertising, you can't narrowly target your market. And you can't be sure that readers will even glance at your ad; they may skip past it to that article on wool-gathering without it even registering.

If you want to go with print ads, you might do better to advertise in the lifestyle or travel section of a metropolitan newspaper in a city in which your guests reside. Depending on the city and the paper, you may be able to run a display ad similar to the one in the national magazine for as little as $100.

The innkeepers we interviewed had mixed reviews of print ads. For their first few years, Bruce and Judy Albert in Florida advertised in every publication they could afford but now primarily rely on the web. Bill and Sandra Wayne in Missouri haven't had much response at all from print advertising. "The only print ad that's done well for us is a half-inch display ad in the nearest urban phone book (Kansas City)," they say.

In Texas, David and Marilyn Lewis agree. "We've advertised a little in the newspaper, a joint venture with all the B&Bs here," they explain. "But we don't feel real good about the response."

It's Classified

Whether you choose magazines or newspapers, print ads come in one of two styles: display and classified. Display ads usually feature some sort of graphics combined with the printed word and are found throughout a publication. Classifieds consist solely of the printed word and are found only in the classified section.

Classified ads are far less expensive than display ads, but they're also riskier. Since people generally only turn to the classifieds when they're looking for something in particular, and then only look in that specific section, you run the risk that the casual reader will pass them by entirely.

Bright Idea

David and Marilyn Lewis in Fort Worth, Texas, take guests' photos, add a line on the bottom that says, "We made a memory with" the name of the B&B, and then glue a magnet to the back so guests can stick their reminiscences on their refrigerators—terrific free advertising.

Going Public

Public relations is a terrific source of free advertising. Word-of-mouth is one of the most powerful promotional tools available. When you use these winning public relations techniques, you get people talking about your inn. And that means booking rooms as well as local people referring out-of-town guests to you.

Tip...

Smart Tip

People usually have to see an ad repeatedly before it prompts them to buy. Budget for at least six runs of your ad in a single publication, and don't be discouraged if you don't get much response at first.

You're the Guest

Local groups are always looking for guest speakers. Offer yourself on a free basis to local associations or clubs that match your target audience. Start your brainstorming with these tips for starters:

- Give a talk on your historic home and the history of your neighborhood
- Host a cooking workshop or demonstration
- Lecture on your particular target niche, whether it's gardening, bird-watching, or bicycling
- Offer a how-to session on restoring a historic home
- Give a talk on home decorating, either from a historic or contemporary perspective

Charity Begins with B&B

Not only did the Alberts advertise in every print publication they could afford, but they also advertised by helping worthy causes. "We gave to almost every charity. We still donate room nights to charity, but primarily we advertise on the web."

As an adjunct to internet advertising, donating room nights or gift certificates to charity auctions and fundraisers is terrific publicity. You get your name in front of people—and not just anybody. People who can afford to buy at charity auctions can afford to pay upscale B&B room rates. And once people start to stay at your inn, they'll tell other people, and the word will spread.

And as any successful businessperson in any industry will tell you, word-of-mouth is one of the most important advertising sources you can tap. Don't forget that a guest at your bed and breakfast has an extended network of friends, co-workers, family, and all of their friends, co-workers, and family.

Romancing the Writers

Placing ads is not the only way to get into print. Send news releases (which are also called press releases) to local and regional publications when you host a special event, from a Victorian Christmas to a Midsummer's Eve extravaganza, as well as when you donate gift certificates to charity, or give a talk or workshop.

You'll have to be creative because editors are inundated with materials—many of which are mind-numbingly uninteresting. But news releases can be extremely effective free advertising. Not only will potential guests read about you, but you can put "as seen in *Toledo Today Magazine*" on your brochure—which looks terrific.

News releases take the form of one- or two-page articles, usually accompanied by a photo or two. Try these tips for news release success:

- *Craft your release to sound like news instead of advertising.* Editors want to read and publish hard copy—they're not in business to give you a free plug.

- *Keep your release short and concise with a cutting edge of interest.* Tailor a news release, for instance, about your stress-free weekend getaways to tie in with current concerns about health problems from stress.

- *Tailor your release to the publication.* Write a release on country cooking for culinary magazines; tweak it to emphasize using herbs instead of salt for a health publication or a magazine for seniors.

- *Follow the standard news release format.* Start off with a catchy lead, or opening, followed by hard but fascinating facts. Double-space your copy. Keep the font of your news release easy to read—this is not the place to experiment with quirky typefaces.

- *Call the magazine, and ask which editor your release should be addressed to.* Get correct name spellings and addresses.

- *If your release is time-sensitive—for instance, it will describe holiday decorating at your inn—make sure you submit it on time.* Magazines often work three to six months ahead of the cover date, so you may need to have that Christmas article on the editor's desk by July.

- *Follow up.* Wait a few weeks, then call the editor to make sure she's received the release, and ask if she has any questions. Then be persistent—if your first release, doesn't make print, try again with a new one.

> ## Bright Idea
> Think about what your inn could sponsor to help a good cause—if you've got a stunning garden, you might give out ribbons for a city beautification project; if your niche is offering crafting workshops, volunteer to judge a local competition.

Inn the Money

Managing Your Income

Just as your house needs periodic checkups to make sure the air-conditioning filters are clean, the septic tank isn't overflowing, and the termites aren't feasting on the framing, so do your finances. Financial checkups can reveal, for example, that you're spending too much on direct-mail advertising or on the trappings and treats at afternoon teas. Or they can divulge that you're doing great, that you can now afford to take on extra help even in the off-season or build that little gift shop next to the driveway.

Reality Check

The first years in the life of your bed and breakfast will typically be the most expensive. You'll have all those start-up expenses, from renovations and a new mortgage to purchasing linens, towels, software, and registering your business name. Fortunately, until the time comes (and it will) that you decide to remodel or upgrade, these are one-time fees. And the next time around, you'll have more income behind you to pay for all those materials, contractors, and permits.

Charting a Course

An income and expense statement, also called a profit and loss statement, charts the revenues and operating costs of your business over a specific period of time. Check out the income statements in Chapter 8 on pages 143 and 144 for our two hypothetical bed and breakfasts, Pieces of Eight and Lightning Bug Bay. Use the worksheet on page 145 to chart your own income statement. Then sit back for a moment and smell the cinnamon rolls.

Living Seasonally

If your income is seasonal—as that of so many B&Bs is—you'll have to get accustomed to making the fat times stretch into the lean. The very fact that you're seasonal will help a little; your utility bills will be lower in the off-season, and so will your food and labor costs.

Still, it can be a shock to people used to having that company payroll check faithfully rolling in every two weeks to realize that there's not much to put in the bank this month. And that there won't be for the next several months to come.

Not to panic. Instead of spending your high-season earnings on frivolities, bank as much as possible; then during the slow season, you can kick back, relax, and recharge your batteries for the hectic summer or winter to come.

Feeding Uncle Sam

There's another hungry mouth besides the snails and caterpillars looking to bite off a chunk of your inn business, and that's Uncle Sam. While you should consult your accountant for the details as they pertain to your specific B&B, you can figure on a few basics when it comes to tax time for the small business.

> **Tip...**
>
> ## Smart Tip
>
> Contrary to popular belief, the IRS can be nice—if you just want a question or two answered. Go online at www.irs.gov to find the toll-free number for your region, then give them a ring.

You can, for instance, deduct the cost of business equipment and supplies, subscriptions to professional and trade journals, and auto expenses. Keep a log of business miles so you can deduct trips to the market, the home improvement center, the garden supply store, and to speaking engagements.

When you travel for business purposes, you can deduct air fares, train tickets, and rental car mileage along with hotels and meals. And you can even—under certain circumstances—deduct recreational side trips you take with your family while you're traveling on business. Since the IRS allows deductions for any such trip you take to expand your awareness and expertise in your field of business, it makes sense to also take advantage of any conferences or seminars that you can attend—a busman's holiday to keep abreast of events in your target market or to see how the competition's doing.

You may also be able to deduct some living expenses, from utilities and your mortgage to remodeling costs, because your home is your business. But because of this fact, you can also get into a lot of trouble with the IRS if you get too creative with the deductions. Ask the advice of an accountant who understands B&B taxes to help you out at tax time—don't wing it. To find an inn-savvy accountant, ask around at the Professional Association of Innkeepers International, your local association or your local reservation service organization.

Plumping Your Pillows

As a savvy innkeeper, there are lots of things you can do to plump up your revenue pillows and increase your income during both high and low seasons. Both seasons, of course, are important, but the more creative you can get with ways to bring in guests during the off-season, the more well-rounded your income will be. Try some of these tips for starters:

- *Oh, murder.* Murder mystery weekends are popular among both hosts and guests. You devise the plot, the murder, and choose the victim; then invite your guests, who can even come in costumes. Mystery weekends usually include dinners. (Remember, if you're not set up or approved for dinner meals, you may able to have them catered. Add the catering fee into your weekend package price.) Purchase a murder mystery in a box at any store that sells board games to get you started—or invent your own.

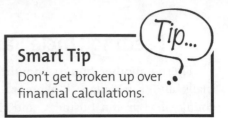

Smart Tip

Don't get broken up over financial calculations.

- *Have-fun how-tos.* Here's where you can use your special expertise—or someone else's. Host a weekend-long workshop on cooking with herbs, painting landscapes, restoring antiques, making topiaries, writing romances, or whatever your target market will be interested in. If you're not an expert, entice someone else to handle the how-to part for you. Authors, for instance, will often jump at the chance to help out while promoting their new book so long as you provide them with an honorarium, room-and-board, and sometimes travel expenses or a small fee.

- *Ah, romance.* Romance sells big in the B&B world. Put together a special package that includes elements like a horse-drawn carriage ride; moonlight cruise; a candlelit, catered in-room supper; a box of chocolates and bottle of champagne; a flower-strewn bath; or a serenading violinist. You can't really go over the top in the romance department, so go creative instead. And make sure you don't miss out on Valentine's Day!

- *Happy holidays.* Brainstorm packages for all sorts of holidays. Go all out for a costumed and decorated period Christmas à la Charles Dickens, the Civil War, the Roaring '20s, or whatever era your house is. Fashion a romantic New Year's Eve gala for two. Host a Halloween bash, and let guests decorate pumpkins, then dress up and dance among the ghosts in your garden. Invite guests to a lucky St. Paddy's weekend with soda bread and bacon on the breakfast table, and a leprechaun's gold scavenger or treasure hunt.

Going for Gifts

Fun Fact

People with green thumbs like to travel to gardens. Almost 40 million Americans recently took a garden tour, visited a botanical garden, or attended a garden show or festival, according to the Travel Industry Association of America.

Another way to bump up your income year-round is by selling gifts and souvenirs. If you've got the room and the inclination, go all the way with a full-fledged gift shop or display counter. Or do as Marilyn and David Lewis in Fort Worth, Texas, do, and place a few carefully chosen collectibles on shelves in guest rooms. Everybody likes to take something home, Marilyn points out, and a vintage china ornament can be a perfect reminder of a stay at your B&B. (And it can also serve as a reminder to come back for another visit.)

The Lewises purchase collectibles at flea markets and garage sales; they're not expensive antiques that guests must debate over purchasing, just bits of nostalgia with the same romantic character as their B&B.

You may choose to offer the same sort of wares, tailored to your inn's ambience. Or you might go with new gift wares—anything from tea cups and T-shirts to whimsical bird houses and elegant bed linens. You'll discover all sorts of fun finds at gift shows, which are held regionally all over the country. Contact the National Specialty Gift Association for times and places. Order up coffee mugs, T-shirts, and tote bags emblazoned with your logo. Look under "Advertising Specialties" in your local phone book to find a vendor who'll do the job for you.

You can also shop till you drop for goodies to sell at local arts and crafts shows. The advantages here are that you're promoting local business—which is fun and will make you popular—and you'll stock one-of-a-kind items. As an added bonus, instead of purchasing those works of arts and crafts, you can sell them on consignment. You don't have to pay anything out-of-pocket.

Local Hang-Out

Another way to plump up your income pillows and help feather your nest is to position your B&B as the place for locals to hang out. Not a place to have a burger

Cookin' Up Proof

Your guests will drool for your chocolate cinnamon buns, chile relleno soufflés, and lemon-thyme muffins. Why not indulge them with a cookbook to take home? Sift together a selection of your favorite recipes. Toss in some prose for leavening—bits of the history of your home or neighborhood or heart-warming or humorous stories from your innkeeping experiences. Put it together with some line drawings with your desktop-publishing software, then take it to your favorite print shop, and have a few hundred copies run off and spiral-bound.

Sell your cookbook on your web site and in your gift corner or shop. And don't forget to send press releases to magazines and newspapers!

and a malted or to sit reading the paper and watching the world go by, but to hold afternoon teas, morning business meetings, or evening club groups.

Who wouldn't want to hold their events at your bed and breakfast? With your quiet and upscale ambience, you'll breathe life into dull conferences. And you can serve your signature sweet rolls for breakfast or lime and salmon in aspic instead of the same old donuts or chicken salad for teas.

The Lewises will launch a variety of locals' events once the main house—still under renovation—is up and running. "The dining room will be all period charm, but also state of the art, so people can plug in modems and have business meetings," they say. To capitalize on the calls they already get from businesses and churches requesting staff meeting space, the couple will add media and conference rooms. "We're going to gear it that way," Marilyn explains. "But we'll also have weddings, teas and receptions, and recitals on the Steinway grand piano in the music room. Some people might stay for the evening, too."

Of course, all this doesn't immediately garner you room sales. But it's revenues. And it helps spread the word. People who meet for their monthly book club get-together or neighborhood business network morning at your inn will tell out-of-town relatives and associates about your stellar surroundings and service. And those out-of-towners will become your guests.

Wedding Bell Greens

Some bed and breakfasts get in the greenbacks by soliciting wedding business, putting together romantic packages that include not only the usual chocolates and champagne, but also the cake, the flowers, the music, and even the minister. This can be a big boost to business. You can charge a lot of money for a wedding package. And unless the happy couple is doing the intimate elopement thing, you'll have the bonus of all those wedding guests to put up in your rooms.

For some innkeepers, this is heaven. They love playing a pivotal role in a couple's most romantic event. "We developed a whole wedding business," says Nancy Helsper in San Diego. Guests get married in the chapel at the same heritage park on which her inn stands, and then have their reception in her Queen Anne mansion. "We got very successful at it," Nancy reports. "That and the corporate business made us."

For other hosts, however, a wedding—while lucrative—is a nightmare. Guests can get rowdy, brides' mums can be cantankerous, and brides can work themselves into hysteria over everything from the cake to the candles.

If you decide to do weddings—or other events from bar mitzvahs to birthdays—ask for a damage deposit, list the specific services and products you'll provide in writing, and then set a payment schedule. Fifty percent when arrangements are set in motion and the other 50 percent due a week prior to the wedding is customary.

Make sure you charge over and above the amount that caterers, florists, cake decorators, and musicians charge you. Acting as a de facto wedding consultant is a major undertaking—don't sell yourself short. Add on at least 10 percent for your time and effort.

Smart Tip

Tip...

Don't forget to set out the visitors book for wedding guests to sign—add those names to your mailing list!

Makeover Magic

Innkeepers are always indulging in some sort of makeover magic for their B&Bs—in part because it's fun, but even more so because it's a way to increase revenues. As you build your business, you'll begin to learn what your guests want in terms of rooms and amenities, as well as which elements have more pull. And you'll remodel (again!) to meet those needs. "There's a constant state of evolution as you develop a property, define your spirit, and meet guests' needs," explains Nancy Sandstrom in Bayfield, Wisconsin.

Nancy and her husband, Steve, for instance, brought their B&B from the four guest rooms it had when they purchased it up to five rooms and one suite. Six years later, they've decided that the smallest room—always the last to book, Nancy says—needs to go.

Daringly Different

The elements that guests want—and will pay the most for—are king-sized beds, whirlpool tubs, and fireplaces. If you can't add these amenities, think about what you can do that elicit the same sorts of oohs and ahs.

A room that opens onto the backyard, for instance, might be transformed into a Charleston or New Orleans-style secret garden room with a privacy fence enclosing lush landscaping and a cafe table for two.

Get creative! Have an artistic friend faux paint a room to look a jungle, forest, or castle in the air; then add furnishings to match. Entwine twinkling lights in inexpensive "silk" ficus trees. Build in a window seat. Make a headboard from picket fencing or a canopy by draping yards of chiffon from the ceiling. Paint stars on the ceiling. Do what guests won't dare to do themselves at home—and they'll be delighted.

The couple are drawing up plans to convert it into a common room, with a small kitchenette stocked with a tea service, wine glasses, corkscrews, book cases, a guest phone, and a computer modem. Two massage therapists, to whom the inn already refers business, will come in and do on-site massages in the new common room. "We'll offer a higher level of service and amenities," Nancy explains.

The $8,000 drop in revenues from the sacrificed guest room will be balanced out by the fact that, with the new amenities, Steve and Nancy can increase the rates on their remaining rooms. And they'll save on per-room costs like cleaning. "It's a game," Nancy says.

When the Helspers in San Diego purchased their second building, the Italianate villa next door, it had only one large suite. The couple added two more—which worked out beautifully. "People want a fantasy," Nancy says, "and the more, the better. If I could do it all over again, I'd do all suites."

13

Booked Solid or
Bare Rooms

If you've read through this entire book, you know that a bed and breakfast is an overnight success only in the daydreams of aspiring innkeepers. You can definitely flourish, but not immediately and only if you're willing to apply a combination of sheer physical labor, wise money management, savvy sales and marketing, and of course a love of entertaining and nurturing your guests.

To help you with all of the above, we asked the B&B hosts interviewed for this book for advice on making your innkeeping dreams come true.

Advice for the B&B-Lorn

"Research, research, research," Nancy Sandstrom in Bayfield, Wisconsin, exhorts. "Do your homework. This business is so personal that many innkeepers will clamp their mouths shut and not want to tell you their occupancy rates or revenues, so it's hard to know what questions to ask and how to ask them. Use the information available from the Professional Association of Innkeepers International and state associations. Join any state associations—ours was incredible."

Nancy believes in getting your feet wet while you're collecting facts and figures. "I highly recommend asking innkeepers to let you help them by inn-sitting or tagging along for a few days," she says. "Ask if you can shadow someone, and try it out."

"Become an innkeeper if you love to be with people. If you enjoy seeing people have fun, then this is the business for you," David and Marilyn Lewis in Fort Worth, Texas, counsel. "But be willing to do a lot of hard work."

"Get ready to work very hard, and be prepared for every—and any—possible situation," Bruce and Judy Albert in Seaside, Florida, advise. "Have enough money saved to keep you surviving for a couple of years, or have a very rich relative."

In Warrensburg, Missouri, Bill and Sandra Wayne echo this sentiment. "Have enough money or other income to get through a couple of years without an operating profit," they say. "Don't make projections too optimistic."

And in San Diego, Nancy Helsper agrees, advising thoroughly defining your income needs and comparing them with your debt service so you don't end up with many harsh surprises.

Martha Stewart's Rival

As we explored at the outset of this book, it takes a certain personality to become a successful innkeeper. You have to combine hosting skills to rival Martha Stewart's with promotional savvy and bookkeeping skills. If this describes you, you'll probably thrive. If not, you may come to the realization sooner or later that instead of having a booked-solid reservations calendar, you're staring at empty rooms. Or your calendar's full, but you're on burn-out circuit overload.

Which is OK; with everything you'll have learned, you'll make a terrific employee. This is another of the terrific things about being self-employed: You can give it up if you want to.

Sweet Dreams

None of the innkeepers interviewed for this book, however, seems to have any intention of giving in and going corporate. They like what they're doing and how they're doing it and plan to keep on hosting.

But can it all be sweet dreams? Even the most experienced and successful hosts must live through the occasional nightmare. To find out, we asked our interviewees about their worst—and best—experiences in the business.

Get Naked

"Our worst experience?" asks Marilyn Lewis in Texas. "That's easy. We had an exhibitionist who wanted to run around naked." And did. Marilyn, who was away from the inn at the time, found out when she received a panic call from her housekeeper. Marilyn called the police, who promptly sent out an officer to investigate. When the law knocked at the guest's door, the man fortunately got nervous and decided to leave. "He didn't stick around," Marilyn says with a laugh. "But he did sign our guest book!"

Bright Idea

Dream pillows are the latest thing for the well-dressed bed. Made of soothing and scented herbs like lavender and chamomile sewn into pillows, they promote sleep and sweet dreams. Why not try a few for your guests?

The Test Drive

Nancy Helsper in San Diego feels her worst experience was during construction of her inn's new suites. "Driving the contractor was very difficult," she says. But urging him on was critical because the new rooms had been presold, which meant construction could not lag behind. "We were literally making the beds five minutes before our first check-in," Nancy remembers. "That's not how you do it. Instead, you should have friends stay in the rooms before you sell them. This is called a 'soft opening.' "

Something Smelly at the B&B

In Florida, Bruce and Judy Albert had a different check-in "worst." They double-booked a room. And in Missouri, Bill and Sandra Wayne experienced a worst of another sort—or smell. "The sewer backed up right before a big holiday tour," Bill recalls.

And Nancy Sandstrom in Wisconsin reports as her worst another smell incident—this one involving smokers. Her B&B was always a nonsmoking house, something about which she feels very strongly, but for the first two years guests were allowed to smoke in the garden. Then Nancy and Steve hosted a group that booked out the entire inn. "And in this particular group," Nancy says, "everyone was a smoker."

Each morning, the entire group woke up, bounded out of bed, and made a beeline for the front porch, where they'd stand and smoke. Smoke drifted in through the screen door, all through the house and into the kitchen where Nancy was fixing breakfast. And fuming. "I don't match with the people in my house," she remembers thinking unhappily.

When the group went off for the day—leaving behind a litter of cigarette butts in the potted plants—Nancy decided that enough was enough. "It was no longer a nonsmoking house," she says. "Now it's a nonsmoking property."

The Best

Nightmares don't last forever, thank goodness, and just as innkeeping isn't always sweet dreams, it isn't all night sweats and monsters under the bed, either. The hosts we interviewed had no difficulties coming up with rewarding moments as well.

Hummingbird Magic

"We've had so many wonderful guests," Nancy Sandstrom says. In fact, going into her sixth year as an innkeeper, there are only five people on her "sorry, we don't have a room if they call back" list. And one of Nancy's very first guests definitely is not on the "sorry" list.

"The first weekend we were open, we had walk-ins, a couple who were driving by and saw us," Nancy recalls. "They were my first walk-ins, and we were their first B&B." The couple spent the night and were at the table when Nancy served breakfast the next morning. "I was scared to death," she remembers.

Despite Nancy's first-day jitters, breakfast went well, and the lady half of the walk-in couple strolled out to the porch. In a few moments, she was back. Her face aglow, the woman told Nancy that she had been sitting on the porch swing when a hummingbird flew down and

> **Fun Fact**
> The first Bible-in-a-hotel-room-drawer was tucked into place at the Superior Hotel in Montana by Gideons International in 1908.

hovered, wings fluttering, right beside her for probably 20 seconds—which is a very long time for hummingbirds. "That means good luck," the woman told Nancy. "It's symbolic of what you have here; it's such a special place."

It was a moment that Nancy treasures. "It's in the way we approach our guests, the way we clean our rooms, and arrange the food on our plates," she says. "It taught me an important lesson. Everyone should have a hummingbird fluttering in their ears."

The Nicest Couple

"We've had so many best experiences," Marilyn Lewis says. "When we have new guests, I tell David, 'Aren't they the nicest couple?' But then I always say that because they are."

In addition to all the marvelous people who've come through their doors, David and Marilyn have also hosted a few very special guests. A friend of theirs occasionally foots the bill for deserving couples to stay at the inn, and she always insists on anonymity. The couples have no idea of their benefactress' identity. "The husbands of two couples were terminally ill," Marilyn says. "And the third couple have seven adopted children and needed a rest. Our friend always says, 'I wonder who I'll send to you next?'"

The Psychic Paycheck

Bill and Sandra Wayne count their best experience as making new friends on a regular basis. Bruce and Judy Albert say, "It's enjoying the appreciation shown us by the many guests who have passed through our doors."

And Nancy Helsper expresses similar emotions. "Every day when I serve breakfast, I get a psychic paycheck from my guests," she says. "They tell me they love their room, and they're glad to meet me."

Nancy describes a recent breakfast where two of her guests were a charming 80-year-old who was celebrating her birthday at the inn along with her daughter. "Everybody loved the woman at breakfast," Nancy recalls. She was a delight. After the meal, the daughter took Nancy aside and explained that her mother had only three months to live. "'Thank you so much for this memory,' the daughter told me," Nancy recalls. "Every day someone says thank you. Which makes all the paperwork worth it."

On Your Own

If, after everything you've learned in this book, you decide to go for it on your own, you'll soon collect a scrapbook full of your own worst and best experiences to share. But if you go into innkeeping with the right ingredients—a willingness to work hard, to learn everything you can, the confidence to promote yourself and your B&B, and the drive to succeed—chances are you will thrive.

Appendix
Bed & Breakfast Resources

The quintessential pantry for the successful innkeeper is filled not just with biscuit mix, flour, sugar, jams, and jellies, but with a wealth of resources—a master list of places to go and people to contact for information on everything from industry associations to reservation services. We've compiled a list of resources to get you started stockpiling your own information pantry.

These sources, however, are starters. They are by no means the only sources out there, and they should not be taken as the ultimate answer. We've done our research, but businesses—like people—do tend to move, change, fold, and expand. So as we've repeatedly stressed, do your homework. Get out, and get investigating. Don't be afraid to ask questions. You'll be amazed at how much you'll learn!

Associations

American Society of Home Inspectors,® Inc., 932 Lee Street, Suite 101, Des Plaines, Illinois, 60016, (800) 743-ASHI (2744), fax: (847) 759-1620, www.ashi.org

National Mail Order Association, 2807 Polk St. NE, Minneapolis, MN 55418-2954, (888) 496-7337 (for ordering books and reports only), (612) 788-1673, www.nmoa.org

Professional Association of Innkeepers International, 207 White Horse Pike, Hadden Heights, NJ 08035, (856) 310-1102, www.paii.org

Note: Check out the extensive list of state and regional B&B associations at www.travel guides.com/innkeepescorner/assoc.html

B&B Guide Web Sites

Bed and Breakfast.com, www.bedandbreakfast.com

Bed & Breakfast Inns Online, www.bbonline.com

Pamela Lanier's Travel Guides Online, www.travelguides.com

Select Registry, Distinguished Inns of North America, www.selectregistry.com

Books

Breakfast in Bed California Cookbook, Carol Frieberg, Sasquatch Books

How to Open and Operate a Bed & Breakfast, Jan Stankus, Globe Pequot Press

How to Start and Operate Your Own Bed and Breakfast, Martha Watson Murphy, Owl Books

How to Start and Run Your Own Bed & Breakfast Inn, Ripley Hotch and Carl Glassman, Stackpole Books

Open Your Own Bed & Breakfast, Barbara Notarius and Gail Sforza Brewer, Chronicle Books

So You Want to Be an Innkeeper, Mary E. Davies, Pat Hardy, Jo Ann M. Bell and Susan Brown, Chronicle Books

Helpful Government Agencies

Bureau of the Census, www.census.gov

U.S. Postal Service, www.usps.com

Note: Be sure to contact your own and state health departments for any rules and regulations you may need to know.

Innkeeping Software

Easy InnKeeping, Grace Software Inc., P.O. Box 42237, Houston, TX 77242-2237, www.gracesoft.com

InnReserve International, www.innreserve.com

RezOvation LLC, 700 Brazos St., Suite 8700, Austin, TX 78701 (866) 565-1000, www.rezovation.com

Inn Sales

Aardvark & Associates Inc., P.O. Box 594, Odessa, FL 33556, (813) 265-2419, (888) 707-4626, www.inns forsale.com

InnKeepingForSale.com, 250 Magog Rd., Appleton, ME 04862, www.innkeepingfor sale.com

Reservation Service Organizations

Bed & Breakfast Reservations, 11 Beach Rd., Gloucester, MA 01930, (781) 964-1606, (978) 281-9505, www.bbreserve.com

Mi Casa Su Casa, Advance Reservations Inn Arizona, P.O. Box 950, Tempe, AZ 85280-0950, (800) 456-0682, (480) 990-0682, www.azres.com

Nutmeg Bed & Breakfast Agency, P.O. Box 271117, West Hartford, CT 06127-1117, (800) 727-7592, (860) 236-6698, www.BnB-Link.com

Successful Bed & Breakfasts, Cottage on the Knoll at Cedarcroft Farm, Bill Wayne, 431 Southeast County Rd. Y, Warrensburg, MO 64093, (660) 747-5728, www.cedarcroft.com

Heritage Park Inn, Nancy and Charles Helsper, 2470 Heritage Park Row, San Diego, CA 92110, (800) 995-2470, (619) 299-6832, www.heritageparkinn.com

Josephine's, Bruce and Judy Albert, 338 Seaside Ave., P.O. Box 4767, Seaside, FL 32459, (850) 231-1940

Lockheart Gables Inn, David and Marilyn Lewis, 5220 Locke Ave., Fort Worth, TX 76107, (817) 738-5969, (888) 224-3278, www.lockheartgables.com

Pinehurst Inn at Pikes Creek, Nancy and Steve Sandstrom, 83645 State Hwy. 13, Bayfield, WI 54814, (715) 779-3676, www.pinehurstinn.com

Glossary

ADA: *see* Americans with Disabilities Act

Americans with Disabilities Act: federal law concerned with making public buildings and areas accessible to disabled people

Architectural review board: governing body that regulates architectural and decorative codes for a city, neighborhood, or subdivision

Assignment: clause in a real estate sales contract that allows the buyer to assign the contract to another legal or personal entity

Availability calendar: reservation calendar made available to guests on an inn's web site

Bed and breakfast: lodging establishment with a live-in owner and four to eight guest rooms that offers breakfast as part of the room rate

Bed-and-breakfast inn: lodging establishment with a live-in owner and six or more guest rooms that offers breakfast as part of the room rate

Bed-and-breakfast hotel: hotel with 30 or more rooms that offers breakfast as part of the room rate

Bed tax: a tax levied by cities or counties on guest room rates

Certificate of occupancy: certificate issued by the building department that gives a property owner permission to inhabit a newly built or renovated building

Compiled list: a mailing list composed of people in specific categories, e.g., doctors, lawyers, Manhattan residents

Country inn: lodging similar to a bed-and-breakfast inn except that it also features a restaurant open to the public

Current replacement value: in insurance terms, the amount it would cost to replace an item if purchased new at current market rates

dba: see fictitious business name statement

DIY: do-it-yourself remodeling or repairs

Fictitious business name statement: the name a business legally registers for itself

Focus group: a group of people gathered for the purpose of conducting market research

General contractor: contractor who hires and supervises subcontractors like roofers, framers, or tile installers

Ground-fault interrupter (GFI): electrical outlet for bathrooms, kitchens, spas, and other water-prone areas to prevent accidental electrocution

Homestay: private home with one to four rooms for paying guests

Inn-sitter: baby-sitter for an inn

List broker: a company or individual specializing in mailing-list rentals

Loan origination fee: percentage of a mortgage or other loan paid to the bank to be granted the loan

Market niche: the segment of a market in which you plan to excel

Mechanic's lien: lien placed on a property by a contractor or other worker who hasn't been paid

Occupancy: the number of guest rooms filled on a daily basis

Overbook: to reserve the same room for the same night for two different sets of guests

Reservation service organization: agency that makes reservations and handles bookings for member B&Bs

Response list: a mailing list composed of people who have previously responded to a specific mail-order campaign; for instance, people who buy from garden catalogs or people who stay at hotels

Roll-over service: telephone feature that permits a busy line to roll, or switch, over to an idle one

Room night: one night's lodging for one guest

RSO: *see* reservation service organization

Selects: specific categories, such as age, geographic region, or income bracket, by which names on a mailing list can be sorted and selected for mailings

Shoulder season: season ranked in terms of occupancy rates between high season and low season, typically spring or fall

Soft opening: testing a guest room for flaws before selling it to the public by having friends or family stay in it for free

Subcontractor: a contractor specializing in a particular building trade like plumbing, electrical, or framing

Tariff: rate

TDD: see telecommunications display device

Telecommunications display device: device that gives the hearing-impaired telephone access

Turn-down service: to turn down blankets and bed linens for pampered guests to slip into

Unhosted apartment or cottage: self-contained lodging separate from the host's home in which breakfast is offered as part of the room rate

Index